Parenting Teen Boys with Confidence

A Therapist's Guide to Building Resilience, Independence, and Self-Esteem in Young Men

Laura Thomas M.Ed.

© **Copyright 2024 - All rights reserved.**

The content contained within this book may not be reproduced, duplicated or transmitted without direct written permission from the author or the publisher.

Under no circumstances will any blame or legal responsibility be held against the publisher, or author, for any damages, reparation, or monetary loss due to the information contained within this book, either directly or indirectly.

Legal Notice:

This book is copyright protected. It is only for personal use. You cannot amend, distribute, sell, use, quote or paraphrase any part, or the content within this book, without the consent of the author or publisher.

Disclaimer Notice:

Please note the information contained within this document is for educational and entertainment purposes only. All effort has been executed to present accurate, up to date, reliable, complete information. No warranties of any kind are declared or implied. Readers acknowledge that the author is not engaged in the rendering of legal, financial, medical or professional advice. The content within this book has been derived from various sources. Please consult a licensed professional before attempting any techniques outlined in this book.

By reading this document, the reader agrees that under no circumstances is the author responsible for any losses, direct or indirect, that are incurred as a result of the use of the information contained within this document, including, but not limited to, errors, omissions, or inaccuracies.

Table of Contents

INTRODUCTION: READY, SET, PARENT LIKE A PRO! 1

CHAPTER 1: DECODING THE BOY BRAIN 7
- WHAT'S GOING ON IN THERE? 8
- INSIDE THE TEENAGE BRAIN 11
- EXPLAINING THE GRUNTS 15
- WHAT THIS MEANS FOR YOU 19
- PRACTICAL TIPS 20

CHAPTER 2: FINDING HIS TRIBE 27
- FINDING PURPOSE IN THE WORLD 28
- FINDING THE "RIGHT" FRIENDS 31
- INFLUENCE OF ROLE MODELS 35
- IMPACT OF SOCIAL MEDIA AND INFLUENCERS 39
- PRACTICAL TIPS 41

CHAPTER 3: MATES, DATES, AND HEARTBREAKS 47
- INITIATING THE CONVERSATION ABOUT RELATIONSHIPS 48
- TEACHING ABOUT RED FLAGS IN RELATIONSHIPS 51
- #COUPLEGOALS 56
- GETTING REAL ABOUT FEELINGS 58
- ENCOURAGING OPEN COMMUNICATION WITH PARENTS 61
- PRACTICAL TIPS 62

CHAPTER 4: CHILL OUT, DON'T LASH OUT! 69
- GETTING A GRIP ON EMOTIONS 69
- WHAT REALLY SETS THINGS OFF 72
- TALKING IT OUT WITHOUT FREAKING OUT 74
- TURNING FIGHTS INTO INSIGHTS 76
- ANGER OR ADHD? 77
- PRACTICAL TIPS 78

CHAPTER 5: LET'S TALK ABOUT ADDICTION 85
- UNDERSTANDING ADDICTION 85
- SCREEN TIME OR SCREEN TRAP 88
- PARTY TIME: THE REALITY OF DRUGS AND ALCOHOL 92
- SEX AND PORN 95
- PRACTICAL TIPS 98

CHAPTER 6: MENTAL HEALTH MATTERS KNOW THE SIGNS.................................105

- Understanding the Silent Struggles... 105
- When Anger Is a Cry for Help... 109
- Spotting the Subtle Signs of Self-Harm... 112
- Starting the Conversation About Mental Health....................................... 116
- Promoting Mental Wellness 119
- Practical Tips... 121

CHAPTER 7: LEVELING UP— GETTING READY FOR ADULTHOOD 125

- The Journey to Adulthood... 125
- Breaking Free From the "Be a Man" Mentality.. 129
- Building Self-Esteem From the Inside Out... 131
- Encouraging Independence and Self-Reliance 134
- Finding Purpose and Passion 136
- Practical Tips... 138

CHAPTER 8: "PARENTS AREN'T PERFECT" A TEEN'S GUIDE TO YOU 143

- Seeing Ourselves Through Their Eyes 143
- Breaking Down the Barriers 145
- Adapting Your Parenting Style 147
- Connecting Through Their World... 149
- The Need for Parental Self-Reflection 151
- Practical Tips... 153

BONUS CHAPTER: PARENTING HACKS 157

- Building Confidence... 158
- Managing Emotions 160
- Improving Communication... 162
- Encouraging Positive Behavior 163

CONCLUSION 167

GLOSSARY 169

ABOUT THE AUTHOR 171

REFERENCES.. 175

To my wonderful teenage girls, Amy and Charlotte, and my endlessly supportive husband, Phil—thank you for showing me just how fulfilling and meaningful parenting can be.
To my clients—the remarkable teens and their parents I've had the privilege to work with—your resilience and stories continue to inspire me daily. Thank you for letting me be a part of your journey

Introduction:
Ready, Set, Parent Like a Pro!

I'm so worried that he'll feel I failed him or, even worse, that he's failed himself—just the thought that I might have let him down, not prepared him for life, or that he could end up on the wrong path scares me to my core.
–Rebecca, mum of two teen boys

These words echo the fears of so many of the parents I've worked with over the years. The raw honesty in her confession touches on a universal truth of parenting teens: We're all terrified of somehow letting our children down during these important years.

Rebecca's not alone in her worries. I've sat across from countless parents who've shared their deepest fears about their teenage sons. Some are terrified their boys will fall in with the wrong crowd, taking a path that leads to trouble. Others lie awake at night, their minds conjuring up the worst-case scenarios of their sons making one bad decision that lands them in serious trouble or even prison.

These fears might seem extreme, but they come from a place of love and a deep desire to see our children thrive. They also stem from the utterly baffling experience of parenting a teenage boy.

One minute, your son is this sweet, curious kid asking a million questions about the world, and the next, he's grunting one-word answers and rolling his eyes so hard that you worry they might get stuck that way.

Maybe you picked up this book because you're feeling a bit overwhelmed, confused, or just in need of some guidance. Well, you've come to the right place. As a psychotherapist who works with teens and parents, I'm here to share what I tell parents in the therapy room—and trust me, there's a lot to unpack!

My name is Laura, and I'm going to share the insights I've gained from my years of experience working with teens and families (and from raising my own teens!). You're going to hear stories (with names changed, of course) that might sound eerily familiar to what you're currently going through. We're going to laugh together and maybe even shed a tear or two, but most importantly, we're going to learn how to build stronger, more understanding relationships with our boys.

I'm here to remind you that you are not alone. Parenting a teenage boy can be challenging and unpredictable, and sometimes, it might feel downright impossible. Parenting a teenage boy can also be incredibly rewarding. You just need the right tools and mindset!

There's a lot of focus these days on empowering girls (which is fantastic, don't get me wrong), but sometimes it feels like our boys are being left behind. They're growing up in a world that's more connected and complex than ever before, facing pressures and challenges that we, as parents, might not always understand. That's why this book is all about championing healthy structures for boys—helping them understand the world, their role in it, and how to be assertive because their opinions matter.

So, what can you expect from this book? Well, I hope you didn't come here expecting a typical parenting book. We're going to dig deeper than just telling you to take deep breaths when your son's room looks like a disaster zone (though that can help, too!).

Instead, we're going to explore the following together:

- **The teenage brain:** I'll simplify the complexities of neuroscience into practical advice. When you understand what's going on in your son's head, you can be better prepared to work through those mood swings, impulsive behaviors, and his seemingly never-ending search for identity.

- **Social pressure in a digital age:** Our kids are growing up in a world that's more connected than we ever imagined when we were young. We'll talk about how to help your son handle peer pressure, online influences, and the constant fear of missing out

(FOMO). As parents and guardians, we might not always be around to offer guidance on these things, but we can work with our kids to set up safe structures for healthy interactions online and in their relationships, helping them set boundaries and make smart decisions independently.

- **The family setup:** You really do need all the help you can get, so we'll discuss how to create a supportive environment where your son feels heard and valued.

- **Mental health matters:** Raising resilient young men with a positive outlook is crucial, but we also need to be careful not to push them too hard. We'll explore how to balance encouragement with understanding.

- **Practical strategies:** Each chapter will end with actionable tips you can start using right away. These are like your parenting cheat codes!

Just so you know, this journey isn't just about your son; it's about you, too! Parenting is a journey in which we are constantly growing and learning alongside our kids. Here's a secret I want to let you in on early: You are actually allowed to make mistakes, have doubts, and sometimes feel like you have no idea what you're doing. That's all part of the process.

If you're feeling nervous about turning the page and getting started, I want you to take that deep breath I mentioned earlier and remind yourself that millions of parents have survived teenage boys before you. They didn't have me to guide them through, so you're already 10 steps ahead!

Let's get started in Chapter 1 by decoding the boy brain. I promise it's going to be a lot of fun and also educational.

PRINTABLE

Boost Your Teen's Confidence with

TWO FREE Journals!

As you explore *PARENTING TEENAGE BOYS WITH CONFIDENCE*, give your teen a head start with *UNSTOPPABLE YOU* and *CONFIDENT YOU*—two powerful journals designed to boost self-esteem, emotional awareness, and mindful growth!

What's Inside Each Journal:

- **Mood Trackers** to encourage self-awareness.
- **Feel This, Try This** guides for managing emotions.
- **Goal Planners** to inspire focus and ambition.
- **Mindful Coloring** for relaxation
- **Reflection Prompts** to build confidence.

CHAPTER 1:

Decoding the Boy Brain

It's Saturday morning, and you're standing in the doorway of your teenage son's room. The scene before you is nothing short of apocalyptic—clothes strewn everywhere, dishes growing their own ecosystem, and in the middle of it all sits your son. He has his headphones on and is completely oblivious to the chaos surrounding him. You call his name once, twice, three times... Finally, he looks up, grunts something that sounds vaguely like, "What?" and then returns to his game.

Do you remember when I said you're not alone? This is one of those scenarios that feels almost universal. I say "almost" because not all teen boys are the same. The universal part is really that we've all found ourselves wondering, "What on Earth is going on in that head of his?"

Well, you've come to the right place! In this chapter, we're going to be looking into the mysterious and often baffling world of the teenage boy brain. We'll explore the developmental stages your son is going through, from the early years of childhood to the cusp of adulthood. We'll also unpack what's really happening inside that brain of his—learning why he seems to have forgotten how to use full sentences, why risk suddenly seems so appealing, and why, the love of all that is holy, he can't seem to remember to put his dirty socks in the laundry basket.

It's fascinating stuff! But we're not only here to satisfy our curiosity; we're actually going to be equipping ourselves with the knowledge we need to parent effectively during these important years. When we understand what's driving our son's behavior, we can respond with empathy, set realistic expectations, and provide the support they need to work through this challenging period of time.

What's Going On in There?

Let's begin by taking a look at the developmental stages your son has been through and is heading toward. This is like your map, starting with the "why" stage of early childhood to the "why not" stage of the teenage years.

Overview of the Developmental Stages

Each of these stages comes with its own set of challenges and opportunities for growth. Let's break it down (Cleveland Clinic, 2023; *Development of Self*, n.d.; Griffith University, 2014; van Schoor, 2023):

Early Childhood (2–7 Years)

This is the "little scientist" phase. Do you remember when your son was constantly asking "why" and trying to understand the world around him? This stage is so important for language development, imagination, and the beginnings of logical thinking. It's when boys start to develop their sense of self and begin to understand that other people have thoughts and feelings, too (even if they don't always act like it in their teenage years!).

Challenges: The challenge here is often managing that endless curiosity and energy. Your son might test boundaries constantly, which can be exhausting.

Opportunities for growth: This is also a fantastic opportunity to nurture his love of learning and help him develop emotional intelligence.

Middle Childhood (7–11 Years)

This is often called the "golden age" of childhood. Your son was likely more independent, developing stronger friendships, and becoming more aware of his place in the wider world. This stage is key for developing problem-solving skills, a sense of industry, and the ability to think more abstractly.

Challenges: Friend drama often starts here, and academic pressures might increase.

Opportunities for growth: This is a great time to help your son develop a strong work ethic and build resilience.

Early Adolescence (11–14 Years)

This is when things get wild, and puberty kicks in, bringing a whole host of physical, emotional, and cognitive changes. Your son might start to challenge authority more, seek greater independence, and become hyper-aware of his social status among his peers.

Challenges: Mood swings, anyone? This stage can be tough as your son starts to pull away and assert his independence.

Opportunities for growth: The silver lining? It's a crucial time for him to start developing his own identity and values.

Middle Adolescence (15–17 Years)

The wildness continues... but now with an extra dash of WTF. This is often the peak of risk-taking behavior, identity exploration, and the infamous teenage mood swings. It also happens to be a time of significant cognitive development, with his abstract thinking skills becoming more sophisticated.

Challenges: Risk-taking behaviors peak here, which can be nerve-wracking for parents.

Opportunities for growth: This is also when many teens start to develop passions and think seriously about their futures.

Late Adolescence (18–21 Years)

This is the final stretch before adulthood. Your son is likely to be thinking more about his future, developing a stronger sense of identity, and (hopefully) gaining more emotional stability.

Challenges: The challenge here is often letting go and allowing your son to make his own decisions (and mistakes).

Opportunities for growth: It's also exciting to see him start to become the adult he'll be.

Why is it so important for us parents to understand these stages? Well, imagine trying to go on a road trip without a map or GPS. Sure, you might eventually get where you're going by looking at the road signs, but you'll probably take a lot of wrong turns and experience a fair bit of frustration and stress along the way. Your understanding of these signs is your GPS for your son's growth. It helps you know what to expect and understand why certain behaviors are happening. Then, you can figure out how best to support your son through each phase.

Understanding these stages also helps us to tailor our parenting approach to what our sons need at each point in their development. When your 13-year-old suddenly starts spending hours in front of the mirror and worrying about what his friends think, you'll know if it's not just vanity or peer pressure—it's a normal part of developing his identity and social awareness.

Or when your 16-year-old makes a decision that leaves you scratching your head, you'll understand that his brain is still developing impulse control and long-term thinking skills. Now, be warned: This knowledge doesn't necessarily make the behavior less frustrating, but it can help us respond with patience and understanding rather than exasperation.

Just as a bit of a disclaimer here: Not all kids are going to fit perfectly into this framework. Every child is unique. Some are going to hit milestones earlier or later than others, and that's okay. Use this as a guide, not a strict rule book.

Inside the Teenage Brain

Now, we're going to venture into the complex, sometimes chaotic world of the teenage brain. In the early teenage years, the brain undergoes significant growth and development, and knowing this is crucial for understanding teen behavior and emotional responses. Don't worry; I'm going to walk you gently through this neurological jungle. There's no need to be afraid of the science!

The Prefrontal Cortex

Let's start with the prefrontal cortex, aka the brain's CEO. This is the part that's responsible for all those "adulting" skills we're trying to instill in our teens—things like decision-making, impulse control, planning, and thinking about consequences (*Brain Development in Pre-Teens and Teenagers*, 2021). In teens, this part of the brain is still very much under construction.

You can imagine your son's prefrontal cortex as a young intern, eager but inexperienced, trying to run a Fortune 500 company. He's got potential, but he's going to make some questionable decisions along the way. This is why your normally smart, capable teen might do something breathtakingly foolish, like thinking it's a good idea to skateboard off the garage roof into the pool (true story from one of my clients—don't worry, the boy was fine. I can't say the same for the skateboard or the mom's blood pressure!).

The prefrontal cortex doesn't fully mature until the mid-20s (*The Teen Brain: 7 Things to Know*, 2020). So when we're asking our teens to "think before you act" or "consider the consequences," we're literally asking them to use part of their brain that isn't fully operational yet. It's like asking someone to drive a car that's still on the assembly line—that would be a bumpy ride!

The Limbic System

Next up, let's talk about the limbic system, the brain's emotional center. This includes structures like the amygdala, which processes emotions and forms memories. This is where things get interesting: While the prefrontal cortex is still developing, the limbic system is already in full swing (Murdock, 2020).

Think of it as a seesaw, with logic and emotion on opposite ends. In the adult brain, this seesaw is fairly balanced. But in the teen brain, the emotional side is sitting pretty while the logical side is still climbing up. This imbalance is why teens often react emotionally to situations that adults can approach more rationally.

Take a moment to think about the last time your son had an emotional meltdown over something that seemed trivial to you, like not being able to find his favorite shirt. That's his limbic system in action, processing emotions at full throttle while his prefrontal cortex is still learning to apply the breaks.

Hormonal Changes

As if the brain remodeling wasn't enough, let's throw some hormones into the mix! During puberty, the brain is flooded with hormones like testosterone and estrogen—it's like someone poured rocket fuel into your son's emotional engine.

These hormonal surges can lead to increased aggression, mood swings, and risk-taking behaviors (Monroe, 2012). They're also responsible for the physical changes your son is experiencing, which can be a source of pride, embarrassment, or anxiety—sometimes all in the same day!

One moment, your son might feel like he's on top of the world, ready to take on any new challenge that comes his way. The next, he might be overwhelmed by self-doubt or irritation. It's not just your son being dramatic—his brain is literally on a chemical roller coaster.

Dopamine and Reward Sensitivity

Up next, I want to talk about the brain's "feel good" chemical, dopamine. During adolescence, there are significant changes in the brain's reward system. Teens actually have lower baseline levels of dopamine, but they experience bigger surges of it in response to pleasurable stimuli (França & Pompeia, 2023; Galvan, 2010).

So, what does this mean in practice? It means that teens are wired to seek out new, exciting, and potentially risky experiences. That video game that your son can play for hours is giving his brain little dopamine hits every time he levels up. The dare from his friends that makes you want to bubble-wrap him for safety is also an irresistible opportunity for a dopamine rush.

This heightened sensitivity to reward also makes teens more vulnerable to addiction and impulsive behavior (Romer, 2010). It's why they often prioritize immediate gratification over long-term goals. The idea of studying for a test next week? Boring! Staying up late to chat with friends? Well, that's the dopamine jackpot!

Sleep Patterns and Brain Development

Maybe you've noticed that your teen is staying up later and later but then struggling to drag himself out of bed in the morning. Yeah, you are not alone there. Adolescence brings a shift in circadian rhythms, pushing teens towards a later sleep-wake cycle (Hagenauer et al., 2009).

This isn't your son being difficult (although it might feel that way when you're trying to get him to school on time). His brain is actually releasing melatonin, the sleep hormone, later at night and keeping it elevated longer in the morning.

The trouble is that while his internal clock is shifting, the external world often doesn't accommodate this change—hello, school start times! The result is a chronically sleep-deprived teen, which can affect everything from academic performance to emotional regulation.

Here are a few practical tips to help manage teen sleep habits:

- Encourage a consistent sleep schedule, even on weekends.

- Create a calm, screen-free bedtime routine.

- Ensure the bedroom is dark, quiet, and cool.

- Limit caffeine, especially in the afternoon and evening.

Good sleep isn't just about quantity; it's actually really important for brain development, memory consolidation, and emotional processing (*What the Science Tells Us about Adolescent Sleep*, n.d.).

Social and Environmental Influences

Last but certainly not least, let's talk about the social brain. During adolescence, peer relationships take center stage. Your son's brain is hyper-tuned to social cues, making him more susceptible to peer influence—both positive and negative (*Environmental Factors Impacting Teen Mental Health*, 2024).

This increased social sensitivity is why your teen might be obsessed with his social media presence or why a seemingly minor social rejection feels like the end of the world. It's also why peer pressure can be so powerful during these years.

However, it's not all bad news here. This social sensitivity also means that teens have an increased capacity for empathy and social connection. It's a prime time for them to develop deep friendships and learn important social skills that will serve them throughout life.

Your job is to help your son work through these influences. Encourage positive peer relationships, help him develop strong values, and be there as a sounding board when he needs to process social situations.

To be clear, understanding all of these different aspects of the teenage brain doesn't excuse poor behavior, but it does help explain it. More importantly, it gives you an understanding of how to support your son through this crazy time.

Explaining the Grunts

I'm sure you're familiar with the teenage grunt—that monosyllabic response that can mean anything from "Leave me alone" to "I'm starving" to "The world is ending, and I don't know how to tell you."

So, how can we turn those grunts into actual conversation?

Understanding Teen Communication Styles

First things first: Why do our once chatty kids suddenly turn into grunt machines? Well, there's more going on here than meets the ear.

The Biology Behind the Grunt

Think back to all that brain development we talked about earlier because it plays a big role here, too. The language centers in the brain are going through their own renovation during adolescence (Ciccia et al., 2009). Sometimes, your teen might struggle to find the right words to express complex emotions, hence the grunt.

Emotional Overload

Teens are dealing with a tsunami of emotions, often all at once. When we ask them, "How was your day?" we might be opening a floodgate they're not ready to handle. A grunt or a shrug can simply be their way of saying, "I'm not sure I can process all this right now."

The Need for Privacy

As teens start to form their own identities, they often feel a strong need for privacy. Those one-word answers might be their way of creating emotional space and asserting independence.

Social Pressure

I hate to break it to you, but in the world of teens, being too open with parents isn't always "cool." Some teens might minimize communication with parents as a way of fitting in with peers.

The "You Don't Understand" Syndrome

Many teens feel that their parents can't possibly understand what they're going through. Rather than try to explain and risk feeling misunderstood, they might opt for the safer route of saying as little as possible.

Effective Communication Strategies

Now that you understand a bit more about why our teens might be challenging their inner cavemen, let's talk about how to foster more open communication with them (kirriliesmout, 2015; Pizzini, 2015):

Speak Their Language

For the record, I don't mean that you should grunt back at them (though sometimes it might be tempting!). Instead, try communicating in ways that feel natural to them. Text messages, for example, can sometimes elicit more responses than face-to-face conversations. One mom I worked with started sending her son funny memes related to his interests—it became their way of connecting.

Create a Judgement-Free Zone

Teens often clam up because they fear facing criticism or lectures. Make it clear that they can talk to you without fear of immediate judgment or punishment. This doesn't mean there are no consequences for their actions, but it does mean you'll listen first and react later.

Ask the Right Questions

Instead of "How was your day?" which is usually going to get a dreaded "Fine" and nothing more, you can try asking more specific questions. Try asking, "What made you laugh today?" or "What was the most interesting thing you learned?" These can help you bypass the grunt reflex and encourage more thoughtful responses.

Use Side-by-Side Communication

Many teens, especially boys, are more comfortable talking when they're not making direct eye contact. Try striking up conversations during car rides, while working on a project together, or while taking a walk.

Validate Their Feelings

When your son does open up, do your best to resist the urge to immediately problem-solve or dismiss his concerns. Responses like, "I can see why that would be upsetting" or "That sounds really tough" can go a long way in making them feel heard and understood.

Be Patient and Persistent

Always remember that good communication is a marathon and not a sprint. Keep making efforts to connect, even if you are met with grunts and eye-rolls. Your persistence shows that you care and that you'll be there when they're ready to talk.

Share Your Own Experiences

Teens often think that their parents can't possibly understand what they're going through—as if you were never actually a teen yourself, right? Sharing your own teenage experiences (yes, even the embarrassing ones) can help bridge that gap and make you more relatable.

Respect Their Privacy

While it's important to keep those lines of communication open, it's equally as important to respect your teens' need for privacy. Knock before entering their room, don't snoop through their things, and ask before sharing their information with others.

Use Humor

A little humor can go a long way in diffusing tensions and opening up communication. Just be careful that your jokes aren't at your teen's expense—I find that self-deprecating jokes often work the best.

Be Available

Sometimes, you might find your teen wants to talk at the most inconvenient of times—like when you're trying to meet a work deadline or it's way past bedtime. Try to be as available as possible when they are ready to open up because these moments are golden opportunities for connection.

Every grunt, eye-roll, and shrug is a form of communication. Our job as parents is to be patient decoders, always ready to listen when our teens are ready to talk. It's not always easy, but with persistence and understanding, you can turn those grunts into conversation and strengthen your bond with your teenage son.

What This Means for You

So, what does all this mean for you and your day-to-day parenting?

Your teenage son is in a tricky spot—he's not a child anymore, but he's not quite an adult either. He needs your support, but he also craves independence. It's like he's learning to ride a bike all over again, but this time, the bike is life, and you're not allowed to hold the seat.

Here are some tips for striking that balance:

- **Gradual independence:** Give him opportunities to make decisions and face consequences in low-stakes situations. Maybe he chooses his own study schedule or manages his own laundry. If he fails, it's a learning opportunity, not a disaster.

- **Safety-net parenting:** Be there to catch him when he falls, but don't prevent him from taking risks. Your role is changing from a manager to a consultant.

- **Celebrate effort, not just results:** With their still-developing prefrontal cortex, teens might not always make the best decisions. Acknowledge their efforts to think things through, even if the outcome isn't perfect.

- **Patience is key:** Your son's brain is still under construction. What seems obvious to you might not be clear to him yet. Take a deep breath and remind yourself that this, too, shall pass.

Now let's look at some overarching strategies for helping to create a supportive environment that will foster healthy communication:

- **Open door, open mind policy:** Make it clear that your teen can come to you with anything, anytime. No judgment, no immediate lectures—just open ears and an open heart.

- **Family rituals:** Establish regular times for connection, like family dinners or weekend outings. These provide natural opportunities for communication.

- **Respect privacy:** Knock before entering his room and ask before posting about him on social media. Showing respect for his space and privacy can encourage him to be more open with you.

- **Model good communication:** Share your own thoughts and feelings. If you want him to open up, you need to do the same.

- **Create a "Yes" environment:** Look for opportunities to say "Yes" instead of always saying "No." I am not telling you to be permissive here, but suggesting that you find positive ways to meet his needs and desires.

Good communication isn't just about talking; you have to create an environment where your teen feels safe, respected, and understood.

Practical Tips

You've reached my favorite section of the chapter. This is where you get your cheat sheet for working with the teenage boy brain. It's a culmination of everything we have learned throughout the chapter, in short, powerful tips (Dent, 2020):

Understand the Transition

It's so important to remember that your son's brain is still under construction, especially in areas related to decision-making, impulse control, and emotional regulation. Your job is to practice patience and empathy, recognizing that he may not fully understand or control his emotions and actions.

What NOT to do:

- Don't expect adult-level decision-making or emotional control.
- Don't punish or criticize harshly for impulsive behavior.
- Don't assume he's being difficult on purpose.

What TO do:

- Offer patience and understanding when he struggles with emotions or decisions.
- Explain the brain changes he's going through to help him understand himself better.
- Provide guidance and support in developing decision-making skills.

Pause and Respond Calmly

When faced with challenging behavior, take a moment to breathe and respond thoughtfully. Reacting with frustration or anger can escalate situations.

What NOT to do:

- Don't react immediately with anger or frustration.
- Don't engage in shouting matches or heated arguments.
- Don't make decisions or dole out punishments when emotions are high.

What TO do:

- Take a deep breath and count to 10 before responding.
- If needed, take a short break to calm down before addressing the issue.
- Model calm behavior and emotional regulation.

Avoid Nagging

I know it's really hard when you have no forks and the cups are growing their own ecosystem, but instead of going into his room to criticize the mess or complain about untidiness, try to limit your comments about his behavior. Teens often feel overwhelmed by constant criticism, leading to more grunts, eye rolls, and resistance.

What NOT to do:

- Don't repeatedly point out the same issues (like a messy room) multiple times a day.
- Don't use sarcasm or exaggerated sighs to express your frustration.
- Don't make sweeping generalizations ("You never clean up after yourself").

What TO do:

- Choose specific times to address issues calmly.
- Focus on the most important issues and let minor ones slide.
- Offer to help problem-solve if there's a recurring issue.

Know the Difference in Sensory Perception

Be aware that teenage boys may literally not notice certain smells or messes as adults do because their sensory processing can differ at this age.

What NOT to do:

- Don't assume he's being lazy or deliberately unhygienic.
- Don't shame or embarrass him about body odor or messiness.
- Don't expect him to notice or be bothered by the same things you are.

What TO do:

- Gently point out hygiene issues in a private, matter-of-fact way.
- Explain the importance of cleanliness for social situations.
- Help establish routines for personal hygiene and room cleaning.

Engage in Conversations

Focus on talking about things other than just behavior and cleanliness. Show interest in his hobbies, friends, and passions.

What NOT to do:

- Don't interrogate or rapid-fire questions at him.
- Don't dismiss or belittle his interests.
- Don't force conversation when he's clearly not in the mood.

What TO do:

- Ask open-ended questions about his interests.
- Listen actively without judgment.
- Share appropriate stories from your own teenage years.

Choose Your Battles Wisely

Prioritize what truly matters and avoid turning every small issue into a conflict.

What NOT to do:

- Don't nitpick every small infraction or mistake.
- Don't create rigid rules for every aspect of his life.
- Don't escalate minor issues into major confrontations.

What TO do:

- Decide which issues are truly important for his safety and well-being.
- Let go of minor annoyances that don't have long-term consequences.
- Involve him in setting household rules and expectations.

Encourage Self-Awareness and Reflection

Help your son understand his own development and encourage reflection on his behavior.

What NOT to do:

- Don't lecture or preach about self-improvement.

- Don't compare him negatively to others or to your own teenage self.

- Don't dismiss his feelings or perspectives.

What TO do:

- Share age-appropriate information about brain development.

- Encourage journaling or other forms of self-expression.

- Ask reflective questions to help him process his experiences and emotions.

Lead With Empathy

When addressing behavior, start with empathy rather than criticism. Acknowledge his feelings and perspectives to create a safe space for open dialogue.

What NOT to do:

- Don't start conversations with accusations or criticism.

- Don't dismiss or minimize his feelings.

- Don't assume you know exactly what he's thinking or feeling.

What TO do:

- Begin discussions by acknowledging his perspective.

- Use "I" statements to express your concerns.

- Show that you're trying to understand, even if you don't agree.

These strategies won't work perfectly every time, and that's okay. The key is consistency, patience, and unconditional love. As you move forward, keep in mind that this is all just a phase—a critical, sometimes chaotic, but ultimately, beautiful phase of growth. Your son needs your understanding and unwavering support now more than ever. In the next chapter, we're going to start breaking down how you can help your son find his position in the world during the chaos.

CHAPTER 2:

Finding His Tribe

I want you to picture a teenage boy; we'll call him Tyson. Tyson is sitting on his bed, scrolling through social media for the umpteenth time today. He sees pictures of his classmates at a party he wasn't invited to, his teammates celebrating a win without him (he missed practice to study for a big test), and various influencers seemingly living perfect lives. With each swipe, he feels more and more like he doesn't belong anywhere.

Who am I supposed to be? he wonders, tossing his phone aside with a sigh.

This is the period of time in their lives when all teenage boys are trying to find their place in the world, which is why this chapter is devoted to one of the most important aspects of your son's development: identity formation and the search for belonging. We'll explore how your teen is working to figure out who he is, where he fits in, and what he believes in. It's a journey that's equal parts exciting and terrifying—for both him and you!

As parents, our role in this process is vital and also tricky. We need to be there to support and guide him but also step back and let him explore and make his own choices, and yes, that also means letting him make mistakes. It's a delicate balancing act.

Don't worry, though; I'm going to walk through it with you.

Understanding and supporting your son through this stage isn't just about making his life easier, although that's certainly a bonus. It's actually about helping him to build a strong foundation for his future self. The fact is, the identity he forms now will shape his decisions, his relationships, and his overall well-being for years to come.

Let's see if I can give you a whole new perspective on your son's journey and your role in it.

Finding Purpose in the World

Do you remember when your son was little, and his biggest identity crisis was deciding whether he wanted to be a firefighter or a dinosaur when he grew up? Ah, those were simpler times, weren't they? Now, he's grappling with much bigger questions: Who am I? Where do I fit in? What do I believe?

Welcome to what psychologist Erik Erikson called the "Identity vs. Role Confusion" stage of psychosocial development.

Erikson believed that during adolescence, the main task is to figure out one's identity (Ragelienė, 2016). It's like your son is trying on different hats, seeing which ones fit and which ones make him feel like, well, him. This process isn't always smooth or pretty. There might be days when he comes home with a new hairstyle you're not too fond of or suddenly decides he's a vegan (right after you've done the grocery shopping and meal-planning, of course).

This exploration is normal and necessary. Your son needs to try on different identities to figure out which one truly fits. It's through this process that he'll develop a strong sense of self and his place in the world.

So, what does this mean for you as a parent? It means providing a safe space for this exploration. It also means being open to the changes you see, even if they make you a bit uncomfortable. Most importantly, it means offering unconditional love and support, no matter what "hat" he is wearing today.

Stepping Out of the Comfort Zone

Comfort zones are cozy, aren't they? The problem with comfort zones is that nothing grows there.

So, encouraging your son to step out of his comfort zone is absolutely important for his identity formation. Now, I'm not saying you need to push him into skydiving or public speaking if it's not his thing, but what you should do is gently nudge him to try new experiences, meet different people, and explore various interests. But let's be honest: Getting a teenager to start a new hobby when they've got their Xbox and iPhone practically glued to them can feel like an uphill battle!

I've seen this firsthand with the teens I work with. Let's take the Cordova family. One of the teens tries everything that comes his way and has developed a strong sense of self and confidence through doing so. On the flip side, his younger sibling is the complete opposite, perfectly content chilling in his room and connecting with friends online. Both approaches are valid, and both teens will find their way—just through different paths.

So, what's a parent to do? The key is to offer opportunities without forcing the issue. Gently nudge him to try new experiences, meet different people, and explore various interests. It could be as simple as joining a new club at school, volunteering in the community, or trying a hobby he's always been curious about but nervous to start. Each new experience is a chance for your son to learn more about himself—what he likes, what he's good at, and what challenges him.

Now, when you're met with the inevitable grunt or "I ain't doing that," don't get discouraged. Instead, get curious. Try to understand what's holding him back. Is it fear? Not knowing anyone? Lack of confidence? Understanding the root of his resistance can help you address his concerns more effectively.

It's important to remember that if your teen decides to stay in his comfort zone for now, that's okay, too. He's in a safe space, and opportunities to branch out will come naturally through school, college, and beyond. Your job is to make opportunities available and provide support when he's ready to take them.

Each new experience, whenever it comes, is a chance for your son to learn more about himself—what he likes, what he's good at, and what challenges him. But stepping out of one's comfort zone can be, well, uncomfortable. This is where you come in. You are the one cheering him on and providing a safe place to come back to. Encourage him to take risks, but also let him know that it's okay if things don't work out.

The goal is always growth and self-discovery—perfection shouldn't ever come into it.

It's also equally important to encourage introspection and self-reflection. After he has new experiences, engage him in conversations. Ask open-ended questions like, "What did you enjoy most about that?" or "How did that experience challenge you?" These conversations help him process his experiences and understand how they shape his identity.

Developing Values and Beliefs

As your son explores who he is, he's also figuring out what he stands for. This is the time when teens start to develop their own personal value systems and beliefs.

Now, don't panic if your son suddenly starts questioning the beliefs you've taught him. This questioning is actually a normal and healthy part of identity formation. He's not rejecting you or your values; he's trying to figure out what he truly believes for himself—so try not to take it personally!

Your son's values and beliefs will be shaped by various influences:

- **Family:** Yes, believe it or not, you still have a significant influence! The values you've instilled since childhood form the foundation.

- **Peers:** As we'll discuss more in the next section, friends become increasingly important at this age.

- **Culture and society:** The broader cultural context, including media, plays a role in shaping your son's worldview.

- **Personal experiences:** As your son steps out of his comfort zone, his experiences will inform his values and beliefs.

You do have a role to play in this whole process; you are not just a casual observer here! You are going to act as a sounding board for him and a gentle guide. Engage in discussions about values and beliefs and share your own perspectives while being open to hearing his. If he expresses views that concern you, ask him questions to understand where they are coming from rather than shutting them down immediately.

It's important to keep in mind that your son is not going to emerge from adolescence with a carbon copy of your belief system. Your goal should be to help him develop a system that is authentically his own and one that will guide him through the complexities of adulthood.

Finding the "Right" Friends

Think back to when you were your son's age. I'm willing to bet that was a time when friends were the center of your universe. Well, not much has changed for teenagers.

You can think of your son's friend group as a mirror. Every interaction, every shared laugh, and every inside joke reflects back to him an image of who he is and where he fits in. It's like a real-time feedback loop for his developing identity.

Let's take Tyson, the example we opened this chapter with. When Tyson hangs out with his soccer team, he sees himself as athletic and part of a team. When he's with his debate friends, he feels intellectual and articulate. Each group brings out different aspects of his personality and helps him understand the multifaceted person he's becoming.

It is not just about fun and games. Peer relationships play a crucial role in developing social skills, emotional intelligence, and self-esteem (Danial, 2020). When Tyson's friends appreciate his sense of humor, it boosts his confidence. When they turn to him for advice, he feels valued and mature.

Warning: As great as it sounds, this mirror can sometimes distort. Negative peer interactions can be just as impactful (Danial, 2020). If Tyson is constantly teased about his appearance, it might lead to insecurity. If his ideas are frequently dismissed, he might become hesitant to share his thoughts.

Toxic Friendships

What if my son falls in with the "wrong crowd"?

I know you've had that thought before. Probably even a few times! This is one that keeps many parents I work with up at night. A bad group can lead a teen down all sorts of roads.

My first tip for this: Take a deep breath. This is a valid concern, but panicking about it isn't going to help anyone. Instead, let's talk about how to identify potentially toxic friendships and what you can do about them.

Familiarize yourself with the following signs of unhealthy peer relationships (Lehman, 2024; Toussaint, 2014):

- He seems anxious, depressed, or withdrawn after spending time with these friends.

- Your son's behavior changes dramatically when he's with or after seeing certain friends.

- His grades start slipping or he loses interest in activities he used to enjoy.

- He's secretive about what he does with these friends or where they go.

- He's engaging in risky behaviors he wouldn't normally consider.

If you notice these signs, it's time to take action. But please, for all that is holy, do not storm in like a bull in a china shop—that rarely works with teenagers! Instead, you could try these strategies:

- **Open a dialogue:** Instead of criticizing his friends, ask open-ended questions about what he enjoys about spending time with them.

- **Express your concerns calmly:** Use "I" statements like, "I'm worried about you because I've noticed..."

- **Encourage self-reflection:** Ask questions that prompt him to think critically about his friendships. "How do you feel about yourself when you're with them?"

- **Set clear boundaries:** If certain behaviors are non-negotiable for you, make that clear. But also be willing to compromise on less critical issues.

- **Provide alternatives:** Encourage involvement in positive activities where he can meet other peers.

You have to keep in mind that outright forbidding a friendship will often backfire, making the relationship seem more appealing instead of less. You have to keep an eye on him while giving him leeway and guiding him toward recognizing unhealthy relationships on his own.

Encouraging Positive Peer Connections

That's the heavy stuff out of the way for now! Let's move on to encouraging positive friendships. After all, that's what we really want for our sons, isn't it?

Things you can do:

- **Encourage involvement in constructive group activities:** Think about sports teams, clubs, and volunteer groups. These are all great places for your son to meet like-minded peers. They provide built-in common interests and often have adult supervision, which can help with building that positive environment.

- **Host gatherings:** By inviting your son's friends over, you not only get to know them but you also provide a safe, supervised space for socializing.

- **Teach and model social skills:** Spend some time discussing the qualities of a good friend with your son. You can even share stories from your own life about friendship challenges and how you overcame them.

- **Encourage diverse friendships:** Exposure to peers from different backgrounds can broaden your son's perspectives and enhance his social skills through experience.

- **Support budding friendships:** If your son mentions a new friend, show interest. Offer to drive them to a movie or help to arrange a hangout.

- **Respect his choices:** As long as the friendships are healthy, try to be open-minded about friends who might not be your first choice. Your son is learning to juggle his own social world.

- **Be a friendship role model:** Let your son see you maintaining your own healthy friendships. It's a powerful, often overlooked way of teaching social skills.

If your son's choice of friends baffles you, know that you are not the first and nor will you be the last parent to tell me that! That kid with the blue mohawk might turn out to be a straight-A student with a heart of gold, while the clean-cut boy next door could be a negative influence. Try to keep an open mind and judge based on actions and impact, not appearances.

Influence of Role Models

We've all heard the idea that children learn more from what you are than what you teach. Well, guess what? Just because your "child" is now taller than you and has a deep voice, that doesn't suddenly stop being true. Role models are extremely important in shaping your son's identity, values, and behavior.

I'm going to bring Tyson back again (sorry, Tyson!) Let's imagine him again; only this time, he's looking around his world for clues about what it means to be a man. He's like a sponge, soaking up examples of masculinity from everywhere—and I do mean everywhere. From his dad, uncles, teachers, coaches, celebrities, and even characters in video games.

Boys particularly need strong, positive male figures in their lives. Why? Because they're trying to answer some big questions:

- What does it mean to be a man in today's world?
- How should a man handle emotions?
- What does a healthy relationship look like?
- How can I be strong without being aggressive?

Positive male role models can provide living answers to these questions. They show boys that it's possible to be strong and sensitive, successful and ethical, confident and humble.

So, how can you make sure that your son has access to good role models?

- **Look close to home:** Family members, teachers, coaches, or community leaders can be excellent role models.
- **Highlight everyday heroes:** Point out men in your community who are making a positive difference.

- **Discuss media representations:** When watching TV or movies together, talk about the male characters. What do you admire or dislike about their behavior?

- **Encourage mentorship:** Programs like Big Brothers or local mentoring initiatives can connect your son with positive male figures.

- **Be mindful of his interests:** If he's into sports, introduce him to athletes known for their sportsmanship. If he loves music, find musicians who use their platform for positive change.

Remember, a role model doesn't have to be perfect (we'll get to that in a moment). They just need to demonstrate qualities you'd like your son to emulate.

When Role Models Disappoint

So what happens when role models fall from grace?

Let's say that Tyson has idolized a certain athlete for years. He has posters on his wall, wears the guy's jersey, the works. Then, scandal hits. The athlete is caught cheating, or worse. Tyson is devastated, confused, and angry.

What do you do?

First, take another one of those handy deep breaths. This is actually an important learning opportunity. Here's how to handle it:

- **Acknowledge the disappointment:** It's okay to let your son know that you understand why he's upset.

- **Separate the person from their actions:** Discuss how good people can sometimes make bad choices.

- **Use it as a teachable moment:** Talk about the consequences of the role model's actions. What could they have done differently?

- **Emphasize values over image:** Remind your son that true role models are defined by their character, not their fame or success.

- **Encourage critical thinking:** Ask your son what he thinks about the situation. This helps him develop his own moral compass.

When you are discussing role models with him, you have to strike a balance. You want to acknowledge the severity of their mistakes without completely demonizing them. This can help your son to learn about how all people are complex and that we can learn from both the positive and negative examples that they set.

Parents as Role Models

This might feel a bit uncomfortable to hear but... you are your son's first and most enduring example of adult behavior. And you're probably the most influential role model.

Yes, you, with your bad jokes, your struggle to understand TikTok, and that regrettable incident with the lawnmower that we don't talk about.

This realization can feel like a lot of pressure. I won't blame you if you need to put the book down for five minutes and grab a drink or something. But come back quickly because I'm about to make you feel much better about it!

Being a good role model doesn't mean being perfect. In fact, how you handle your imperfections can be one of the most valuable lessons you teach your son. Here are some ways you can be a positive role model (and I bet you already do some of these!):

- **Model emotional intelligence:** Show your son that it's okay for anyone to express emotions. Talk about your feelings and how to manage them.

- **Demonstrate respect:** How you treat others, like your partner, your colleagues, and even strangers, speaks volumes to your son.

- **Show integrity:** Let your son see you standing up for your values, even when it's difficult.

- **Admit mistakes:** When you mess up (and you will), own it. Apologize sincerely and show how you'll do better next time.

- **Practice self-care:** Show your son that taking care of your physical and mental health is important.

- **Pursue your passions:** Let him see you engaged in hobbies or causes you care about.

- **Be present:** In a world of constant distractions, giving your full attention is one of the most powerful things you can do.

Finding balance here between being a parent and a role model can be tricky. There will be times when you need to enforce rules or discipline, which might not feel very "role-model-like." I've said it before, and I'll say it many times before this book is done, but the key is consistency, consistency, and more consistency. This time, it's consistency between your words and actions. If you preach honesty, but your son catches you in a lie, your credibility is going to take a huge hit.

He is watching you all the time, not just when you're trying to teach him something. The way you handle stress, the way you treat your partner, the way you talk about your boss when you think he can't hear—it all sinks in. It's a big responsibility, but it's also an incredible opportunity to shape the man your son will become.

Impact of Social Media and Influencers

The digital world today means that your son's tribe extends far beyond his school and neighborhood. It's a global community now, accessible at the touch of a screen. Let's learn how this is impacting your son's identity formation.

Take a moment to think back to your own teenage years. Now add a device that allows you to present a carefully designed and touched-up version of yourself to the entire world 24-7. Welcome to your son's reality!

Social media plays a significant role in shaping teen identity. It's a platform for self-expression, a way to connect with like-minded peers, and a source of validation. When Tyson posts a photo and gets likes, it's a boost to his self-esteem. When he shares his thoughts and receives supportive comments, it reinforces his ideas and values.

The downside is that this digital identity comes with its challenges:

Pros:

- opportunity for creative self-expression
- connection with diverse communities
- platform to advocate for causes they care about

Cons:

- pressure to present a "perfect" life
- vulnerability to cyberbullying
- comparison anxiety
- potential for addiction to likes and comments

The World of Influencers

Now, let's talk about a phenomenon that's radically changed the way teens consume content: Influencers! In case you don't know, these are the YouTube stars, Instagram celebrities, and TikTok sensations that your son might be following religiously.

There are many reasons why influencers appeal not just to teens but to adults, too. They offer entertainment, sure, but they also provide a sense of connection and aspiration. When an influencer shares details of their life, it can feel like a friendship to a teen. When they promote a product or lifestyle, it can become the new "must-have" for your son.

However, not all influencers are created equal, and some can promote harmful ideologies or unrealistic lifestyles. Take Andrew Tate, for example. His misogynistic views and promotion of "hustle culture" have raised significant concerns among parents and educators.

So, how can you help your son critically evaluate online content and personalities?

- **Encourage critical thinking:** Ask questions like, "What message is this person promoting? Do you agree with it? Why or why not?"

- **Discuss the business of influencing:** Help your son understand that many influencers are essentially running a business, which can affect the content they produce.

- **Promote diverse perspectives:** Encourage your son to follow a variety of influencers, including those who challenge his viewpoints.

- **Address controversial figures directly:** If your son mentions someone like Andrew Tate, don't shy away from the conversation. Discuss why his views are problematic and how they contrast with your family's values.

- **Be an "influencer" yourself:** Share content you find inspiring or thought-provoking with your son. Model critical consumption of media.

We cannot wish away influencers, or social media for that matter. It's important to understand their impact on our son's journey to identity formation so we can help guide them. All of these gamers, influencers, and so on will get into our teens' subconscious. That's actually okay as long as we are making sure they understand the reality of what life is like and what a true role model should be.

Practical Tips

Now, let's give you a quick hands-on guide to supporting your son's identity formation before we close the chapter!

Recognize His Need to Fit In

Understand that your son is trying to find his place, and fitting in is important to him right now. He may act like he doesn't care, but deep down, he wants to belong.

What NOT to do:

- Don't dismiss or mock his attempts to fit in with his peers.
- Don't force him to conform to your idea of who he should be.
- Don't panic if he experiments with different identities or styles.

What TO do:

- Show empathy and support during this time without pushing too hard.

- Acknowledge his efforts to find his place in the world.
- Help him find healthy ways to belong and express himself.

Provide Positive Male Role Models

Boys often look for male figures to emulate, so ensure your son has access to men who embody the values you want him to develop.

What NOT to do:

- Don't assume he'll automatically look up to certain figures just because you approve of them.
- Don't ignore the influence of negative male role models in the media or in his life.
- Don't forget that you're one of his most important role models.

What TO do:

- Introduce him to family members, teachers, coaches, or community leaders who demonstrate values and behaviors you admire.
- Discuss what healthy masculinity looks like.
- Be a positive role model yourself, demonstrating the qualities you hope he'll develop.

Encourage Hobbies and Group Activities

Support your son in trying new activities and meeting different kinds of people.

What NOT to do:

- Don't force him into activities he's not interested in.
- Don't dismiss his interests, even if they're different from what you expected.
- Don't overload his schedule with too many activities.

What TO do:

- Encourage involvement in activities like sports, clubs, or community groups where he can find camaraderie and build social skills.
- Support him in exploring diverse experiences and meeting different kinds of people.
- Show genuine interest in his hobbies and the skills he's developing.

Deal With Friendships Wisely

Be curious, not critical about his friends and social connections.

What NOT to do:

- Don't criticize his friends directly, even if you don't approve of them.
- Don't forbid friendships outright (unless there's a serious safety concern).
- Don't ignore signs of toxic or unhealthy friendships.

What TO do:

- Ask questions with genuine interest about his friends and what he enjoys about spending time with them.

- Gently guide him by discussing the qualities of good friendships.

- If you have concerns, express them calmly and listen to his perspective.

Engage With His Digital World

Be curious about his online influences and help him manage the digital landscape.

What NOT to do:

- Don't dismiss or belittle his online interests.

- Don't invade his privacy by snooping on his devices without reason.

- Don't ban social media or online activities entirely.

What TO do:

- Ask him about who he's watching online and take an interest in his digital world.

- Encourage him to share what he likes about these influencers.

- Have open discussions about values, behavior, and media literacy.

- Help him critically evaluate online content and personalities.

Create a Safe Space for Conversations

Regularly check in with him about his feelings and experiences without judgment.

What NOT to do:

- Don't interrogate or pressure him to share.

- Don't react with shock or judgment if he opens up about something concerning.

- Don't breach his trust by sharing what he tells you without his permission.

What TO do:

- Make it clear that you're there to listen, not lecture.

- Create opportunities for casual conversations, like during car rides or while doing activities together.

- Respond calmly and supportively when he shares his experiences or concerns.

Model Healthy Relationships

Show him what supportive, respectful friendships and relationships look like through your own social connections.

What NOT to do:

- Don't maintain toxic or unhealthy relationships in your own life.

- Don't speak negatively about your friends or partner in front of him.

- Don't isolate yourself socially.

What TO do:

- Maintain positive connections in your own life.

- Demonstrate how to communicate effectively, resolve conflicts, and support others.

- Involve him in family friendships to show him what healthy social interactions look like.

Throughout this chapter, we've learned how important finding his tribe is to your son's journey to adulthood. There are many influences shaping his emerging identity, from friendships and role models to the complex world of social media.

I don't mean to alarm you, but your role in this process is vital. You can provide him guidance, foster open communication, and model positive behavior to really help him work through this exciting, but challenging time.

CHAPTER 3:

Mates, Dates, and Heartbreaks

You're sitting in the kitchen enjoying that last peaceful coffee before the after-school madness. The front door suddenly slams open, and your 15-year-old son heads straight to his room. You hear muffled sounds that suspiciously resemble crying. After a gentle knock and some coaxing, you learn that his girlfriend of two whole weeks (practically a lifetime in teen years) has broken up with him. Over a text message. Your heart breaks for him, but you're also wondering when he even started dating in the first place and how the heck you are supposed to handle this new development.

This chapter is devoted to teenage relationships, from first crushes to devastating breakups and everything in between.

Mates/friends/buddies—however you refer to them, these relationships are important in supporting grown self-esteem and identity. However, once they get into a romantic relationship, this is where their identity takes another shift as they explore these new dynamics. Any relationship, whether it's with a girl or boy, will follow the same pattern of identity shift. Relationships are really good for continuing the growth of identity but, as parents, we need to keep an eye out that the relationship remains safe and positive.

So, with that in mind, we'll explore how to initiate those awkward (but important) conversations about relationships and sex, how to help your son understand modern dating, and how to support him through the inevitable ups and downs. We'll talk about healthy relationships, red flags to watch out for, and how to help your son develop emotional intelligence that will serve him well in all his relationships, romantic and otherwise.

You might be feeling a bit out of your depth here—dating has changed quite a bit since our teen years! However, your guidance during this time is more important than ever. Your values, life experience, and unconditional love are exactly what your son needs as he sets out on this new phase of life.

Initiating the Conversation About Relationships

I think it's safe to say that talking to your teenage son about relationships and sex probably ranks up there with getting a root canal on your list of "fun things to do." It's awkward, it's uncomfortable, and you might be worried about saying the wrong thing or overstepping boundaries.

The thing is, though, your son needs this information, and more importantly, he needs it from you. Yes, he could get it from his friends or the internet, but do you really want those to be his primary sources of relationship advice?

So why is this conversation so hard? Well, for starters, it forces us to confront our own discomfort with these topics. Maybe you were raised in a household where these things weren't discussed openly. Maybe you're worried about embarrassing your son (or yourself). Or maybe you're just not sure where to start.

Whatever the reason, it's important to push past our discomfort. Your son needs a safe, judgment-free space to talk about these issues, and you're the best person to provide that.

By the way, creating that safe environment starts with your attitude. You should approach these conversations with openness, honesty, and a willingness to listen. Let your son know that no topic is off-limits and that you're there to support him, not to judge or lecture.

Timing and Approach

Now, my advice is actually not to sit your son down for a formal "birds and bees" talk. That approach might just send him running for the hills faster than you can say "puberty."

Instead, you can look for natural openings in everyday situations. If you ever find yourself watching a movie with a romantic subplot, that's a great opportunity to ask, "What do you think about how that character handled the situation?" Or if you hear a news story about a celebrity breakup, you might say, "Breakups are tough at any age. Have any of your friends gone through that?"

The key is to make these conversations a normal, ongoing part of your interactions and *not* a one-time high-pressure event.

As for timing, be attuned to your son's moods and receptiveness. A long car ride can be a great time for these chats because you're in a private space, and the lack of direct eye contact can make things feel less intense. Or maybe your son is more talkative when you're doing an activity together, like cooking or playing a game.

Active Listening and Validation

When your son does open up, your most powerful tool is going to be your ears. Active listening is so important. This means giving him your full attention without interrupting or jumping in with advice right away.

Some techniques for active listening include (Cuncic, 2024):

- Putting away distractions (yes, that means your phone).
- Using non-verbal cues to show you're engaged (nodding, maintaining appropriate eye contact).
- Reflecting back what you're hearing ("It sounds like you're feeling...").
- Asking open-ended questions to encourage him to elaborate.

It is equally as important to validate his thoughts and emotions. I am not telling you to agree with everything he says (teens often say some less-than-intelligent things!), but I am saying that you should acknowledge that his feelings are real and valid.

For example, if he's heartbroken over what seems like a trivial rejection to you, resist the urge to say, "You'll get over it," or "It's not a big deal." Instead, try something like, "I can see this is really painful for you. Rejection is tough at any age."

Conversation Starters and Topics

I've got your back with this one. Feel free to use any of these conversation starters, but do adapt them to your own style so it doesn't sound like you're reading from a script:

- "I've noticed you've been talking about Sarah a lot lately. She seems to be important to you. Want to tell me about her?"

- "That movie had some intense relationship scenes. What did you think about how the characters treated each other?"

- "When I was your age, dating was pretty different. I'm curious about what it's like for you and your friends now."

- "I read an article about teens and sexting. Is that something that happens at your school? What do you think about it?"

- "I want you to know that you can always talk to me about relationships or sex, even if it feels awkward. Is there anything you've been wondering about?"

Now, I want to take you through some common scenarios I've seen with my clients and how you can respond to them:

Scenario 1: Your son tells you he has a crush on someone.

Response: "That's exciting! Tell me about them. What do you like about this person?"

Scenario 2: Your son is worried about asking someone out.

Response: "It's normal to feel nervous. Let's talk through what you might say. Remember, the worst they can say is no, and if they do, it's not a reflection on your worth."

Scenario 3: Your son is upset about a breakup.

Response: "I'm so sorry you're hurting. Breakups are really tough. Do you want to talk about what happened? It's okay if you don't, but I'm here if you need me."

Scenario 4: Your son asks a direct question about sex.

Response: "I appreciate you feeling comfortable enough to ask me that. It's a great question. Let me make sure I understand exactly what you're asking, and then we can talk it through."

You are not always going to have a perfect script to turn to, and you really can't ask your son to wait while you fetch this book and look up your answers. The key is to keep those lines of communication open. Be honest, be respectful, and most importantly, be there. Your son might act like he doesn't want your input, but trust me, he's listening more than you know.

Teaching About Red Flags in Relationships

I'm sure we all want our children to experience the joy and fulfillment of healthy relationships. The problem is, and I'm sure you'll agree, the path to finding those relationships isn't always smooth. This is why it's important to teach our sons how to recognize red flags in relationships—so they can learn how to spot when things aren't healthy.

So, what does a healthy relationship really look like? Well, in a healthy relationship, both partners:

- respect each other's boundaries and individuality

- communicate openly and honestly

- trust each other
- support each other's goals and interests
- feel safe expressing their feelings
- can disagree without fear of retaliation or abuse
- have a balance of give and take

On the other hand, unhealthy relationships often involve:

- constant criticism or put-downs
- attempts to control the other person's behavior or choices
- excessive jealousy or possessiveness
- manipulation or guilt-tripping
- inconsistent or unreliable behavior
- disregard for the other person's feelings or needs

You should really emphasize to your son that these unhealthy behaviors are not normal or acceptable, regardless of who is exhibiting them.

Recognizing Different Forms of Abuse

When we think of abuse, physical violence often comes to mind first. But abuse can take many forms, some of which can be subtle and easy to overlook. Let's break it down (*Domestic Abuse*, 2024):

- **Physical abuse:** This includes any form of physical harm or threat of harm.

- **Emotional abuse:** This can involve constant criticism, humiliation, or attempts to control through fear or guilt.

- **Verbal abuse:** Yelling, name-calling, or using words to shame or control.

- **Digital abuse:** Using technology to bully, harass, stalk, or intimidate. This can include excessive texting, demanding passwords, or sharing private information or images without consent.

Here are some subtle signs that might be overlooked:

- a partner who always needs to know where they are and who they're with

- frequent "jokes" that are actually put-downs

- pressure to constantly be available via text or phone

- guilt-tripping for spending time with friends or family

- making all the decisions in the relationship without considering their partner's input

You may notice the signs of abuse before your son. Love, as they say, is blind, and our sons may not recognize manipulation. Coercive behavior is subtle and chips away over time. Don't be afraid to tell your son what you are noticing. Be prepared for him to get defensive (expect it, even), but by speaking up, you may just be planting a seed or validating something that he is already feeling but doesn't have the language to express.

Empowering Boys to Speak Up

Here's where things can get tricky. Society often downplays or ignores the abuse of boys by girls. There's a stigma that boys should be "tough enough" to handle it or that they should feel lucky to have any romantic attention, even if it's harmful.

This is absolute nonsense, and it's crucial that we make this clear to our sons.

Abuse is abuse, regardless of the gender of the person inflicting it. A girl who constantly belittles her boyfriend, controls who he can talk to, or pressures him into sexual activity he's not comfortable with is being abusive, full stop.

Here are some tips to empower your son to speak up:

- **Validate his feelings:** If he expresses discomfort with a partner's behavior, take it seriously.

- **Challenge stereotypes:** Discuss how societal expectations of masculinity can make it hard for boys to admit when they're being mistreated.

- **Provide a safe space:** Make it clear that he can always come to you without fear of judgment.

- **Teach him it's okay to say no:** Emphasize that setting boundaries and refusing to tolerate mistreatment is a sign of strength, not weakness.

- **Discuss resources:** Make sure he knows about helplines, school counselors, or other support systems he can turn to if he needs help.

Setting and Respecting Boundaries

Personal boundaries are the limits we set for ourselves in relationships. They can be physical (like how much physical affection we're comfortable with), emotional (what we're willing to share), or digital (how much online interaction we want).

Teaching your son about boundaries is crucial. Here's how you can actually do that:

- **Model good boundaries:** Show him how you set and maintain your own boundaries in your relationships.

- **Encourage self-reflection:** Help him identify what makes him comfortable and uncomfortable in various situations.

- **Teach assertive communication:** Practice phrases like "I'm not comfortable with that" or "I need some space right now."

- **Respect his boundaries:** If he says he doesn't want to talk about something or needs privacy, honor that (unless you have serious safety concerns).

- **Discuss consent:** Make it clear that both partners need to enthusiastically agree to any physical activity and that it's okay to change your mind at any point.

The truth is that learning to set and respect boundaries is a skill that will serve your son well in all his relationships, not just romantic ones.

These are all the tools your son will need to work through complex relationships. By teaching him all of this, you are helping him to understand that he deserves to be treated with respect and kindness and that it's okay to walk away from situations that make him feel unsafe or unhappy.

#couplegoals

This is the age of Instagram, TikTok, and Snapchat, and your son's idea of what relationships should look like is likely being formed from watching his favorite influencers rather than from real-life examples.

Let's imagine for a moment that your son is scrolling through Instagram, and he sees post after post of seemingly perfect couples. They're always smiling, always on exotic vacations, and always surprising each other with elaborate gifts. It's enough to make anyone feel like their own relationship (or lack thereof) doesn't measure up.

The problem is that these posts are often carefully edited snapshots that really don't reflect the full reality of relationships. They are the highlight reel, not the behind-the-scenes footage.

This disconnect between perfectly edited posts and reality can lead to the following (Tran, 2021; *How Social Media Shapes Unrealistic Expectations in Children*, 2023):

- unrealistic expectations about what relationships should look like
- feelings of inadequacy or dissatisfaction with their own relationships
- pressure to perform or create "post-worthy" moments rather than enjoying genuine experiences

It's so important to have conversations with your son about the reality of relationships. Here are some points you can discuss with him:

- Every relationship has ups and downs. Those #couplegoals posts don't show the arguments, compromises, or mundane moments that are part of real relationships.

- Different relationships look different. What works for one couple might not work for another.

- The early "honeymoon" phase doesn't last forever, and that's okay. Long-term relationships involve work, communication, and sometimes, tough times.

- It's normal to have doubts or frustrations in a relationship. It doesn't mean the relationship is doomed or that you're doing something wrong.

Encourage your son to really focus on how he feels in his relationship rather than how they look from the outside.

Healthy Social Media Habits in Relationships

When it comes to sharing about relationships online, here are some guidelines to discuss with your son:

- Respect your partner's privacy. Always ask before posting photos or information about them.

- Don't overshare. It's okay to keep some moments private.

- Avoid airing relationship grievances on social media. Conflicts should be resolved privately.

- Remember that likes and comments don't define your relationship's worth.

- Take breaks from social media if you find yourself constantly comparing your relationship to others.

Balancing privacy and openness is key. Sharing some aspects of a relationship can be fun and affirming, but oversharing can put unnecessary pressure on the relationship.

Getting Real About Feelings

Emotions are a big topic here. While the world has made some huge strides in this particular area, our boys are still often expected to "man up" or "tough it out." Amidst this, how are we supposed to help our sons embrace their emotional sides?

Breaking Down Stereotypes About Masculinity and Emotions

The old "boys don't cry" mentality is outdated and harmful. It's time to challenge these stereotypes and show our sons that real strength lies in understanding and expressing their emotions.

The ability to recognize, understand, and manage our own emotions and recognize, understand, and influence the emotions of others all comes under emotional intelligence (Cherry, 2023). Emotional intelligence is crucial in relationships because it allows for better communication, empathy, and conflict resolution.

Talk to your son about how expressing emotions is a sign of strength, not weakness. I know, I know; he doesn't always listen to you these days. It can help to share examples of admired men, like athletes, actors, or leaders who openly discuss their feelings.

Teaching Emotional Literacy

Being open and honest about their feelings, fears, and insecurities is essential for building deep, meaningful relationships. But how do we encourage them to do this?

Well, they need to feel secure in their own self-esteem and in the strength of their relationship. The fear of being laughed at and mocked is real and a huge fear for young men. Encourage them to express their emotions and reassure them that it's okay to feel and show vulnerability.

Identifying and Expressing Feelings

Many boys struggle with identifying and expressing their feelings, but there are ways you can help with this:

- You could try using an emotions chart to help him expand his emotional vocabulary beyond just "good" or "bad."

- Practice naming emotions in everyday situations. "It sounds like you felt frustrated when that happened."

- Encourage journaling or artistic expression as outlets for emotions.

- Teach techniques for managing intense emotions, like deep breathing, counting to 10, or using the "name it to tame it" approach.

It's always best to start the groundwork with techniques like these when kids are younger, but they can help at any age. Your 16-year-old might look at you like you've got two heads if you whip out a cartoon emotions chart, though, so just be careful how you approach these things if you want to be taken seriously!

Modeling Vulnerability

It's important to help boys understand that vulnerability is a strength, not a weakness. Although this may be easier said than done! As parents, we're our children's first and most influential teachers. You can show your son that it's okay to be vulnerable by:

- expressing your own emotions openly. "I'm feeling a bit anxious about this presentation at work."

- admitting when you're wrong or when you don't know something.

- sharing age-appropriate stories about times you've struggled emotionally and how you coped.

- showing that it's okay to ask for help when you need it.

When you demonstrate healthy emotional expression, you give your son permission to do the same.

Building Self-Esteem and Confidence

Self-esteem and healthy relationships go hand in hand. When we feel good about ourselves, we're more likely to choose partners who treat us well and to speak up when something doesn't feel right.

Here are some strategies for boosting your son's self-confidence:

- Praise effort and character, not just achievements. "I'm proud of how hard you worked on that project" rather than just "Good job on getting an A."

- Encourage him to pursue his interests and passions.

- Teach him to reframe negative self-talk into more positive, realistic statements.

- Give him age-appropriate responsibilities to show that you trust him.

- Show unconditional love and support, especially when he's struggling.

When boys are taught not to cry or be vulnerable, anger can become their main form of emotional expression (*It's Good for Everyone When Boys Can Be Vulnerable*, 2022). Good communication is the foundation of any healthy relationship. So it's up to us to teach our boys how to express their needs and wants clearly and respectfully and how to listen actively and empathetically to their partners. Role-playing different scenarios can be another helpful way to practice these skills.

We also need to teach our sons (and daughters) to realize being vulnerable takes courage, and if someone else is opening up, we must be respectful in the same way that we expect them to respect us.

Encouraging Open Communication With Parents

Building trust with your teen isn't something that you can do in a day. It really is a process that's ongoing. This is the key to building that strong parent–child relationship, so you should make time for regular check-ins with your son. No, I am not suggesting that you have formal sit-down talks every Tuesday night. I am suggesting that you make time to talk, and that can be casual conversations during car rides, while preparing dinner, or during a shared activity.

The secret is just to be consistent with it. Make it a habit to ask about his day, his friends, and yes, his romantic interests. But remember that respecting his privacy is equally important. This means you shouldn't snoop through his phone or demand to know every detail of his life.

Instead, you can create that environment where he feels safe sharing voluntarily. Let him know that you are always available to talk (even when you're busy), but don't force conversation if he's not ready.

Being His Safe Space

"How, how, how?" I hear you asking. Well, to be approachable when your son needs advice or support, it's important to manage your reactions—and that includes your facial expressions! If he comes to you with a problem and you immediately freak out, jump into lecture mode, or give him the most horrified look he's ever seen, then he's less likely to open up in the future.

This is also a great time to practice your active listening skills. When he's talking, focus on understanding rather than coming up with a response. Use phrases like, "That sounds tough" or "How did that make you feel?" to show that you are engaged and empathetic.

The tricky part can be when you need to balance guidance with independence. Offer advice when asked, but also encourage him to think through solutions on his own. You might want to ask, "What do you think you should do?" before offering your own suggestions.

Managing Difficult Conversations

When it comes to topics like sex, consent, and safety, it's normal to feel uncomfortable. He was your baby yesterday, right? But remember, if you don't provide this information, he might seek it from less reliable sources.

My advice is to always start these conversations early and revisit them regularly. Use news stories, TV shows, or movies as conversation starters. For example, "What did you think about how that character handled consent in that scene?"

Be honest about your values, but also be prepared to listen to his perspective without judgment. If he shares something concerning, take a breath before responding. Say something like, "I appreciate you telling me this. Can we talk more about it?"

Finally, even if you disagree with his choices, make sure he knows your love and support are unconditional.

Practical Tips

I'm willing to bet this is already your favorite part of every chapter, right? This is the bit where you get those quick, relevant tips that you can start using TODAY.

Initiate Conversations About Relationships

Starting discussions about dating and relationships can feel awkward, but it's crucial for your son's emotional development and safety. Here's how to approach this sensitive topic:

What NOT to do:

- Don't wait for your son to bring up the topic.
- Don't have one big, awkward "talk" and consider it done.
- Don't assume he's not interested in dating just because he hasn't mentioned it.

What TO do:

- Use everyday situations as conversation starters.
- Have ongoing, casual chats about relationships.
- Show interest in his social life without prying.

Script: "Hey, I noticed that show had an interesting take on first dates. What did you think about how the characters handled it?"

Teach About Healthy Relationships and Red Flags

Understanding what makes a relationship healthy or unhealthy is a crucial life skill. You can help your son develop this knowledge by:

What NOT to do:

- Don't assume he'll figure it out on his own.
- Don't focus only on the physical aspects of relationships.

- Don't ignore the possibility that boys can be victims of abuse, too.

What TO do:

- Discuss characteristics of healthy and unhealthy relationships.
- Teach him about all forms of abuse, including emotional and digital.
- Empower him to set and respect boundaries.

Script: "You mentioned Sarah the other day. What do you like about hanging out with her? What do you think makes a relationship healthy?"

Understand Social Media Influences

Social media plays a significant role in shaping teens' perceptions of relationships. Help your son develop a healthy perspective on online content by implementing the following:

What NOT to do:

- Don't dismiss the importance of social media in teens' lives.
- Don't assume he knows that social media doesn't reflect reality.
- Don't ban social media outright.

What TO do:

- Discuss how social media can create unrealistic relationship expectations.
- Encourage critical thinking about online content.

- Model healthy social media habits yourself.

Script: "I saw a post about #couplegoals the other day. It got me thinking—what do you think real relationship goals should be?"

Encourage Emotional Expression

Boys often face societal pressure to suppress their emotions. Counter this by fostering emotional intelligence and openness:

What NOT to do:

- Don't reinforce stereotypes like "boys don't cry."
- Don't dismiss or minimize his feelings.
- Don't expect him to handle emotions the same way you do.

What TO do:

- Validate his emotions, even if you don't understand them.
- Teach techniques for identifying and managing feelings.
- Model healthy emotional expression yourself.

Script: "It seems like you've been a bit down lately. I'm here if you want to talk about it. It's okay to feel upset sometimes."

Work On Open Communication

Creating an environment where your son feels comfortable discussing relationships and emotions is vital. You can do this by:

What NOT to do:

- Don't react with shock or judgment when he shares.
- Don't interrogate him about his relationships.
- Don't breach his trust by sharing his private information.

What TO do:

- Create a safe, judgment-free space for conversations
- Be available and approachable when he needs to talk
- Respect his privacy while maintaining open lines of communication

Script: "I want you to know that you can always talk to me about anything, including relationships. I promise to listen without judgment."

Check In Regularly

Consistent, low-pressure check-ins can keep communication flowing. Here are some tips for how to go about this effectively:

What NOT to do:

- Don't wait for big events or problems to check in.
- Don't make every interaction about relationships or dating.
- Don't invade his privacy or personal space without permission.

What TO do:

- Pop into his room occasionally just to say hi (knock first!).

- Use car rides or walks for casual chats.

- Bring a snack as an excuse to initiate a low-key hang out.

Script: [Knocking on door] "Hey, I made some extra snacks. Want to hang out for a bit? No agenda, just thought we could chat."

I hope you realize that the conversations you have now (however awkward they may feel) are laying the groundwork for your son's future relationships. Stay open, approachable, and consistent, and you will be teaching him not just about dating but about trust and communication—all while building his emotional intelligence!

CHAPTER 4:

Chill Out, Don't Lash Out!

I have another scenario for you: 15-year-old Falko is having what we'll generously call a "disagreement" with his younger sister over the TV remote (ah, sibling love—it's beautiful, isn't it?). Suddenly, faster than you can say, "Netflix password," Falko explodes. The remote goes flying across the room, narrowly missing the family fish tank. Poor Nemo; he's seen things... Falko storms off, leaving a trail of slammed doors and muttered curses in his wake.

This is teenage anger. Here, hormones run high, and patience runs low. Small annoyances can feel like Earth-shattering injustices, and "Let it go" is less of a Disney anthem and more of an impossible dream.

In this chapter, we're going to explore why your sweet little boy sometimes turns into a fire breathing dragon (minus the cool wings), and more importantly, how to help him manage these intense emotions without burning the house down.

Learning how to deal with conflict is an essential skill for teenagers, especially as they develop their self-awareness and learn to form and maintain relationships (*Conflict Management with Pre-Teens and Teenagers*, n.d.).

We're going to look at what's really going on beneath the surface of these angry outbursts—and it's usually not about the TV remote. When we can understand those underlying emotions and triggers, we can help our sons develop healthier ways to express themselves.

Getting a Grip on Emotions

Let's start by understanding the anger iceberg. Anger is the emotion that really needs no introduction. When we see our sons explode in rage, it's easy to think, *Wow, he's really angry*. But anger really is just the tip of that iceberg.

What we see above the surface (the telling, the slamming, the occasional flying TV remote) is just a small part of what's really going on. Beneath the surface lurks a whole mess of other emotions: fear, hurt, insecurity, frustration, and sometimes, a healthy dose of "I have no idea what I'm feeling, but I don't like it."

These underlying emotions are the iceberg underwater base—huge, complex, and potentially Titanic-sinking if we're not careful. (I promise I'll stop with the iceberg metaphor now.)

So why does anger get all the spotlight? Well, for many boys, anger feels safer and more "acceptable" than these other emotions. Society often tells boys that it's okay to be angry but not okay to be scared or hurt. So, they learn to channel all those uncomfortable feelings into anger.

Now, let's talk about biology for a second, and you may remember that we touched on this in Chapter 1. When your son gets angry, his brain goes into fight-or-flight mode. The amygdala (the brain's own little drama queen) sounds the alarm, flooding his body with stress hormones like cortisol and adrenaline (Myler, 2020). Meanwhile, the prefrontal cortex (the brain's responsible adult) is still under construction in teenagers. This means that the part of the brain responsible for rational thinking and impulse control is not very reliable.

The result is a perfect storm of intense emotions and impaired judgment. This is why your son can go from zero to nuclear in three seconds flat.

Recognizing Emotional Triggers

Now that we understand what these feelings really are, let's see if we can uncover what triggers him in the first place.

Helping your son identify his emotional triggers is like giving him a superpower—the ability to see anger coming before it hits. It's not quite as cool as X-ray vision, but it's a lot more useful in day-to-day life.

You can start by encouraging him to get curious about his own emotions. After an angry outburst (once everyone's calmed down and the TV remote has been retrieved from wherever it landed), ask him to think back:

- What was happening right before he got angry?
- What was he thinking?
- Was there a particular word or action that set him off?

Over time, patterns might emerge. Maybe he always gets angry when he feels criticized, or when he's tired, or when his sister gives him that look (you know the one).

Self-awareness is the key here. The more your son understands his own emotional landscape, the better equipped he'll be to work through it.

Developing Emotional Literacy

Emotional literacy is about being able to identify and express emotions accurately (*The Importance of Emotional Literacy and How to Improve Yours*, 2021). Many boys struggle with this, often defaulting to "fine" or "whatever" when asked how they're feeling—you know, the classic teenage emotional vocabulary. Riveting stuff!

To expand his emotional vocabulary, try introducing him to the concept of the "feelings wheel"—a handy tool that breaks down emotions into more specific terms. Instead of just "angry," he might realize he's feeling "frustrated," "humiliated," or "overwhelmed."

You can make this a family game. Try "Emotion Charades" or "Guess the Feeling." Sure, it might earn you some world-class eye rolls at first, but stick with it. The ability to accurately name emotions is a superpower in disguise.

Keep in mind that you can't actually eliminate anger; it's a normal human emotion. Sometimes, it's even useful. We're trying to help him express it in healthier ways.

What Really Sets Things Off

I could probably write a whole book called *Why Did My Son Just Flip Out Over Something Seemingly Trivial?* That one would definitely be a bestseller, right along with *Why Does My Teenager's Room Smell Like That?*

Jokes aside, let's take a look at some common triggers of conflict. Yes, every teenager is different, but there are some usual suspects here (*Dealing With Anger – for 11-18 Year Olds*, 2021):

Misunderstandings and False Assumptions

These two are behind more teenage conflicts than you realize. Imagine for a moment that your son thinks his friend is ignoring him because he didn't reply to a text. In reality, his friend's phone died. Cue the anger, hurt feelings, and possibly a strongly worded follow-up text. It's like a soap opera but with more emojis and less dramatic background music.

Then, we have unmet expectations and perceived injustices. To a teenager, these can feel like the end of the world. "What do you mean I can't go to the party? This is so unfair!" Cue door slam. Remember, in the teen world, not being allowed to stay out until 2 a.m. on a school night is practically a human rights violation.

Insecurities and Past Experiences

Now, we're going a little deeper. Personal insecurities can be like fuel on the fire of conflict. If your son is feeling insecure about his abilities, a simple suggestion might feel like harsh criticism. It's a bit of an emotional minefield. If you say, "Hey, maybe you could try studying this way," what he hears is, "You're terrible at school and will never succeed in life."

His past experiences play a big role, too. If your son has been bullied in the past, he might be quicker to perceive threats or insults where none were intended. It's like his brain has an overactive alarm system—better safe than sorry, but it's exhausting for everyone involved. This is not uncommon, either. How many adults do you know who keep others at arm's length or overreact to criticism?

Identifying Personal Flashpoints

So, how do we figure out what sets off our particular teen? This is all about data collection—no spreadsheets are required, though, so don't worry.

You can encourage your son to keep a mood journal. Before *you* roll your eyes at me, I'm not asking your son to write, "Dear diary, today I felt sad." He can just keep a simple note in his phone about what happened before he got angry. It can be really eye-opening.

Once you start seeing patterns, you can work together on strategies. If he knows that he tends to lash out when he's hungry (hangry), maybe keeping some snacks on hand could help. If criticism is a trigger, you could try agreeing on a code word that means, "I'm trying to help, not attack."

Triggers aren't just going to go away when you notice them; that's about as realistic as expecting a teenager to voluntarily clean their room. However, recognizing them is a great first step in learning to develop healthier responses.

Talking it Out Without Freaking Out

After you've identified the triggers, then comes actually talking about feelings without everyone losing their cool. This can feel a bit like defusing a bomb, but no pressure! I've got some tips to help ease you through:

Active Listening

We've touched on this already, but it really needs to be mentioned here, too. This doesn't mean just nodding along while thinking about what's for dinner, although I know that it can be tempting when you're busy. We're all guilty of it! But you really need to hear what your son is saying—and sometimes, what he's not saying.

Try this: Next time your son is talking, imagine that you'll have to repeat everything back to him verbatim (don't actually do this, though, unless you want to freak him out). This level of focus helps you catch not just the words but the feelings behind them.

Expressing Feelings Constructively

Now, let's talk about how to help your son express his feelings without going nuclear. This is where "I" statements come in. Instead of, "You always ignore me!" encourage, "I feel hurt when I don't get a response to my texts."

You need to help him transform those "you" statements into personal "I" statements. It's not foolproof, but it can help to de-escalate situations quickly.

Finding Common Ground

When conflicts arise, it's easy to fall into an "us vs. them" mentality. But usually, there is some common ground to be found. Maybe you both want him to succeed in school, even if you disagree on how much Xbox time is appropriate.

You can encourage your son to look for shared goals or interests in conflicts. It can sometimes feel a bit like being a negotiator, but instead of world peace, you're aiming for household harmony.

Communication Scripts

And sometimes, simply having a handy script can help. Again, don't memorize these lines like this is a school play, but keep them in mind as go-to phrases when emotions are running high.

Here are a few you can try:

- "I understand you're feeling [emotion]. Can you tell me more about that?"

- "I know this is frustrating. How can we work together to find a solution?"

- I'm not trying to attack you. I'm concerned because..."

It's best to practice these with your son when things are calm. It might feel awkward at first, but it's like any skill: it really does get easier with practice.

Always keep in mind that you are dealing with a teenager and not a United Nations diplomat. Communication is not going to be perfect. But you can help create an environment where feelings can be expressed and heard without World War III breaking out in your living room.

Turning Fights Into Insights

Do you remember when conflicts were simple? When the biggest fights you had to resolve were about who got the last cookie? They were simpler times, weren't they? Well, now we're dealing with teenage conflicts, which are about as simple as quantum physics... on a good day.

Here's a radical idea for you: What if we viewed these conflicts as opportunities instead of problems? Yes, I know that sounds like something off a cheesy motivational poster, but we are onto something here.

Adopting a growth mindset means seeing conflicts as chances to learn and grow (Yeager & Dweck, 2020). It's like turning your home into a real-life classroom, except the lessons are about emotional intelligence instead of algebra.

Encourage your son to reflect after disagreements. Ask questions like, "What did you learn from this?" or "How might you handle this differently next time?"

You can help to look for patterns in recurring conflicts. Does your son always blow up when he feels his privacy is invaded? Does he get defensive when asked about schoolwork?

These kinds of patterns can help lead you to the underlying issues. Maybe the privacy thing is really about feeling respected as he grows up. Maybe the school defensiveness is about fear of failure.

You can use these insights to understand your son better and help him to understand himself. Help him dig through those layers of anger to find the self-awareness buried beneath.

No pressure or anything, but I also want to point out that you are your son's first and most influential model for handling conflicts.

How can you demonstrate healthy conflict resolution? Well, you should practice what you preach. Use those "I" statements we talked about earlier. Show him that it's okay to take a time-out when emotions are running high: "I'm feeling frustrated right now. I need a few minutes to calm down before we continue this discussion."

Finally, admit when you're wrong and apologize. I know that it's tempting to maintain that parental illusion of perfection, but showing your son that it's okay to make mistakes and own up to them is worth its weight in gold.

Anger or ADHD?

How do you know when anger is just typical teen angst and when it might be a sign of something else, like ADHD?

The answer to this one is about understanding and educating yourself. ADHD is not just about being unable to sit still or focus. It can affect emotional regulation. It's like having an internal thermostat that's a bit faulty and sometimes overheats for no apparent reason.

Kids with ADHD might have a harder time managing their emotions, leading to more frequent or intense outbursts. It's not that they are "bad" or "undisciplined." Their brains are just wired a bit differently (Stanborough, 2021).

The tricky part is that many of these symptoms can look a lot like typical teenage mood swings. The universe apparently decided that parenting teens wasn't challenging enough on its own.

To notice the difference between the two, you need to look for patterns. Is the anger persistent and long-standing? Does it seem out of proportion to the situation more often than not? Are there other signs of ADHD, like difficulty focusing or impulsivity?

If you're reading this and thinking, *Oh, boy, this sounds familiar*, then it might be time to consider professional help.

Some signs that it might be time to seek help include (Axelrod, 2016; Stanborough, 2021):

- Anger outbursts that are frequent, intense, or long-lasting.
- Anger that leads to physical aggression or property damage.
- Your son expresses that he feels out of control.
- Anger issues interfere with school, friendships, or family life.

Seeking help is not a sign of failure but a sign of strength. It's a bit like calling in the special forces when your own army (of parenting strategies) needs backup.

There are lots of resources available for ADHD assessment and management. Start with your family doctor or a child psychologist. They can provide evaluations and, if necessary, develop a treatment plan. This might include therapy, coping strategies, and in some cases, medication.

The goal isn't to "fix" your son—he's not broken. It's about giving him the tools he needs to navigate his emotions more effectively. Think of it as upgrading his emotional software to better handle life's challenges.

Practical Tips

Recognize the Anger Iceberg

Remember that anger is often just the tip of the emotional iceberg. There's usually more going on beneath the surface.

What NOT to do:

- Don't dismiss your son's anger as "just being dramatic" or "hormonal."

- Don't assume you know exactly why he's angry without asking.

- Don't try to fix the problem immediately without understanding the underlying emotions.

What TO do:

- Acknowledge his anger without judgment.

- Ask open-ended questions to understand what's beneath the anger.

- Show empathy for the emotions underlying the anger.

Stay Calm in the Face of the Storm

Your calmness can be contagious (in a good way).

What NOT to do:

- Don't tell him to calm down (no one calms down by being told to calm down).

- Don't match his anger with your own.

- Don't take his angry outbursts personally.

What TO do:

- Take deep breaths and model calm behavior.

- Speak in a low, steady voice.

- If needed, take a short break to compose yourself.

Provide a Cool-Down Period

Give him space for his emotions to settle before addressing an issue with him.

What NOT to do:

- Don't force immediate conversation when emotions are high.
- Don't follow him if he walks away to cool down.
- Don't make threats or ultimatums in the heat of the moment.

What TO do:

- Encourage him to take a break when emotions are running high.
- Allow up to 20 minutes for the emotional brain to calm before trying to discuss the issue.
- Provide a safe, quiet space for cooling down.

Teach and Model Healthy Coping Strategies

Help your son develop tools to manage his anger.

What NOT to do:

- Don't expect him to figure out coping strategies on his own.
- Don't dismiss physical activities as a way to release tension.
- Don't assume what works for you will work for him.

What TO do:

- Introduce and practice deep breathing exercises together.

- Encourage physical activities to release tension (e.g., going for a run or punching a pillow).

- Help him identify his own best coping mechanisms.

Communicate Effectively

This one is always so important. Open, honest dialogue is one of your most effective strategies. If your son can come to you with anything, you're winning at life, not just parenting.

What NOT to do:

- Don't interrupt or argue when he's expressing his feelings.

- Don't use sarcasm or belittle his emotions.

- Don't make assumptions about what he's thinking or feeling.

What TO do:

- Use active listening techniques.

- Validate his feelings, even if you disagree with his actions.

- Use "I" statements to express your own feelings and concerns.

Set Clear Boundaries

It's important to establish what behavior is and isn't acceptable, even when angry.

What NOT to do:

- Don't allow destructive or abusive behavior, even in anger.
- Don't set unclear or inconsistent boundaries.
- Don't forget to follow through on consequences.

What TO do:

- Clearly communicate what behavior is unacceptable (e.g., physical violence, verbal abuse).
- Establish and enforce consistent consequences for crossing boundaries.
- Praise positive behavior and efforts to manage anger constructively.

Recognize Potential Red Flags

Be aware of signs that might indicate a need for professional help.

What NOT to do:

- Don't ignore persistent or escalating anger issues.
- Don't assume it's "just a phase" if anger is significantly impacting his life.
- Don't delay seeking help if you're concerned.

What TO do:

- Pay attention to patterns of anger and potential triggers.

- Consider professional help if anger is frequent, intense, or leads to destructive behavior.

- Be open to the possibility of underlying issues like ADHD.

Managing teen behavior is a process, not something that you just do once, and all is fine. You need to be patient and consistent and take a lot of deep breaths—both of you!

CHAPTER 5:

Let's Talk About Addiction

A 16-year-old sits hunched over his gaming console at 3 a.m. on a school night. His eyes are bloodshot, his room is a disaster zone of empty energy drink cans, and he's muttering, "Just one more level," over and over. Meanwhile, his parents are tossing and turning, wondering where they went wrong and if their son has been body-snatched by an alien with a severe video game habit.

Teenage addiction isn't just about substances anymore. These days, our kids can get hooked on everything from social media to online poker. It's like a buffet of potential addictions out there, and our boys are standing in line with empty plates and big appetites.

In this chapter, we're going to explore why teenage boys are particularly susceptible to addiction, how to spot the signs that your son might be veering into dangerous territory, and what you can do to help steer him back on course.

Understanding Addiction

What exactly is addiction? Well, it's not just your son's inability to put down the PlayStation controller or stop checking Instagram every five seconds (although those might be symptoms).

At its core, addiction is a complex brain disorder where a person compulsively engages in rewarding stimuli despite negative consequences (National Institute on Drug Abuse, 2020). It's like your brain's reward system has been hijacked by a very persistent carjacker who keeps driving you to Pleasure Town, even when the road is full of potholes and heading straight for a cliff.

Addiction isn't picky—it can involve substances like drugs or alcohol or behaviors like gaming, social media use, or even excessive exercise. Yes, you read that right—even too much kale and quinoa can be a problem. Who knew?

The key thing to understand is that addiction literally changes how the brain works. It's like your son's brain has been remapped to prioritize the addictive behavior above all else. That Xbox isn't just a game console anymore. To an addicted teen, it might feel as essential as oxygen.

Why Boys Are More Vulnerable to Addiction

I am not picking on boys here, but biology and society sure are. Let's break it down (National Institute on Drug Abuse, 2011; von der Heiden et al., 2019):

- **Biological factors:** Boys' brains are more sensitive to dopamine, the "feel-good" chemical. It's like they're walking around with their pleasure sensors turned up to 11. This makes them more likely to seek out and get hooked on rewarding experiences.

- **Psychological factors:** Society often tells boys to be tough and not show emotions. So, instead of crying it out or talking about their feelings, they might turn to addictive behaviors to cope. They're almost using video games or substances as emotional Band-Aids.

- **Social influences:** Peer pressure is the ultimate teen superpower, and it often pushes boys to take risks and prove themselves. "Come on, bro, everyone's doing it!" is the battle cry of many a bad decision.

- **Delayed self-regulation:** Boys' brains, particularly the part responsible for impulse control and decision-making, mature later than girls, making them more susceptible to impulsive, addictive behaviors.

- **Limited emotional support:** Boys are less likely to seek help for emotional struggles due to cultural stigmas around vulnerability; they often turn to addictive behaviors as a form of self-medication.

All of this combines to make boys more vulnerable to addiction. It's not their fault—it's just the hand they've been dealt. Understanding this can help us better support them.

Recognizing the Signs

So, how do you know if your son is just going through a phase or if he's developing an addiction? Here are some signs to watch out for (*Common Signs & Symptoms of Addiction*, 2019):

- **Neglecting responsibilities:** Homework? What homework?

- **Losing interest in activities they used to enjoy:** "Nah, I don't feel like playing soccer anymore. I'll just stay in my room... forever."

- **Secrecy and lying:** Suddenly, your open book of a son has more secrets than a spy novel.

- **Mood swings:** More ups and downs than a roller coaster.

- **Changes in sleep patterns:** Nocturnal creature, anyone?

- **Unexplained need for money:** The Bank of Mom and Dad is suddenly getting a lot of withdrawal requests.

If you see one or two of these signs, that doesn't necessarily mean that your son is addicted. Teenagers are weird—and I'm qualified to say that; it's kind of their job! But if you're seeing several of these signs consistently, it might be time to dig a little deeper.

Early detection is key with addiction. The sooner you spot potential problems, the easier they are to address.

Screen Time or Screen Trap

The digital world is a place where friendships are forged through fiber optic cables, and battles are won with thumbs. Unfortunately, it's also a place where self-esteem is measured in likes and followers.

Your son might seem more attached to his phone than a Koala to a tree, and it's not because he's avoiding the dishes (although that certainly is a part of it!).

Social media and gaming platforms are designed to be addictive. They're like digital casinos, complete with flashing lights, instant rewards, and the promise of hitting the jackpot—whether that's a viral TikTok or a Fortnite victory royale.

These platforms work by triggering the release of dopamine in the brain. That's right; dopamine is back and it brought reinforcements! Every notification, every level-up, every like is a little hit of this feel-good chemical. It's like your son's brain is at an all-you-can-eat dopamine buffet, and the servers keep bringing out more plates.

But this digital feast comes with a side of consequences:

- **Mental health:** Constant comparison on social media can lead to anxiety and depression. It's like being in a 24-7 popularity contest where the rules keep changing.

- **Sleep:** The blue light from screens can mess with sleep cycles. Before you know it, your son's circadian rhythm is doing the cha-cha slide at 2 a.m.

- **Social skills:** When most interactions happen through a screen, face-to-face communication skills can suffer. It's hard to read body language when everyone's a 2D avatar.

However, I don't want you to think that it's all doom and gloom in the digital world. Let's look at some positives:

- **Global connectivity:** Your son can make friends and learn about cultures from around the world.

- **Access to information:** Need to know the capital of Burkina Faso at 3 a.m.? No problem! The internet is the world's biggest library, open 24-7.

- **Creativity outlets:** From digital art to music production, tech platforms offer endless ways for teens to express themselves.

- **Skill development:** Coding, video editing, graphic design—these are the languages of the future, and many teens are becoming fluent.

- **Support networks:** Online communities can provide support and understanding, especially for teens dealing with niche interests or specific challenges.

- **Educational resources:** From Khan Academy to language learning apps, the digital world is a treasure trove of learning opportunities.

- **Career preparation:** Being knowledgeable about tech can be a huge advantage on many career paths.

Gaming Addiction

Let's take a closer look at gaming first. It's not all bad, by the way. There are some real benefits here, too. But, like anything, too much of a good thing can turn sour faster than milk left out on a hot day.

Signs of problematic gaming behavior (Cleveland Clinic, 2022):

- preoccupation with gaming to the exclusion of other activities
- lying about time spent gaming
- using gaming to escape negative moods
- jeopardizing school, work, or relationships because of gaming

But before you go and throw that console out the window, remember that gaming can have positive aspects too (*Why Your Children Really Should Play Videogames*, 2023):

- **Teamwork:** Many games require collaboration and communication.
- **Problem-solving:** Puzzles and strategy games can boost cognitive skills.
- **Hand-eye coordination:** Those thumbs are getting a real workout!

The key here is balance. You can use these strategies to promote healthy gaming habits:

- Set clear time limits (and stick to them).
- Encourage a mix of solo and multiplayer games.
- Game together as a family (yes, you might have to learn what a "noob" is).

- Ensure gaming doesn't interfere with sleep, homework, or social activities.

Social Media Addiction

Social media can be a double-edged sword for teen self-esteem. On the one hand, it can provide connection and support. On the other, it's a breeding ground for comparison and insecurity.

The constant need for validation through likes and comments can create a feedback loop of anxiety and depression. Don't even get me started on cyberbullying; that's another whole can of worms.

It's important to encourage mindful use of social media:

- **Teach critical thinking:** Not everything on social media is real. That influencer's "perfect" life? Probably has more filters than a Brita pitcher.

- **Encourage real-world connections:** Remind your son that his worth isn't measured by followers. Real friends don't need a Wi-Fi connection.

- **Model good behavior:** If you're constantly scrolling at dinner, you can bet your son will be too.

- **Set up tech-free zones:** The dinner table should be for tacos, not TikTok.

- **Use built-in tools:** Many phones now have screen time tracking and app limits. Use them!

Party Time: The Reality of Drugs and Alcohol

Now let's talk about that red cup at the party. Drugs and alcohol are both age-old temptations that make us wish we could bubble wrap our kids until they're 30. But that's not really an option, and it's probably illegal, so let's see what we can actually do about substance use in the teen world.

Understanding the Appeal

So, why do teens experiment with substances? The reasons are often more complex than we realize (The Partnership, 2017):

- **Curiosity:** Teens are natural explorers. Sometimes, that exploration extends to substances. It's like they're little scientists, but instead of petri dishes, they're using their own bodies as laboratories.

- **Stress relief:** High school can feel like being in a pressure cooker. Some teens turn to substances as a way to let off steam. They're trying to find the "chill" button in all the wrong ways.

- **Fitting in:** Ah, peer pressure—the invisible force more powerful than gravity in the teen world. The desire to belong can make even the most level-headed teen consider things they normally wouldn't.

- **Rebellion:** Nothing says "I'm not a kid anymore," quite like doing something you're explicitly told not to do. It's teenage logic at its finest.

- **Boredom:** Sometimes, it's as simple as having nothing better to do. Idle hands are the devil's workshop, as the saying goes.

Of all of these reasons, peer pressure and belonging are huge. Fitting in can feel like a matter of survival in the teen world. The fear of being left out is so strong that some teens will go against their better judgment just to feel like part of the group.

Effects on the Developing Brain

The teenage brain is a bit like a computer in the middle of a major software update. It's rewiring, restructuring, and generally figuring itself out. When you throw drugs or alcohol into the mix, things get messy.

Short-term effects can include (National Institute on Alcohol Abuse and Alcoholism, 2022):

- impaired judgment (as if teen judgment wasn't already a wild card)

- memory problems (beyond the usual "I forgot to do my homework")

- mood swings (more intense than the usual)

Long-term consequences are even more sobering (National Institute on Alcohol Abuse and Alcoholism, 2022):

- increased risk of addiction later in life

- potential for stunted brain development

- higher likelihood of mental health issues

Having Open Conversations

The million-dollar question is: How do we talk to our teens about this stuff without sounding like a PSA from the 1950s? Here are some strategies you can use:

Keep It Real

Teens have built-in BS detectors. Make sure you give them facts and are not fear-mongering. It's okay to say, "I don't want you to drink because it can mess with your brain development." Don't say, "If you drink, you'll end up living in a van down by the river."

Listen More, Lecture Less

It's up to you to create that safe space for them to ask questions and express their concerns. Sometimes, being a good listener is much more powerful than having all the answers.

Share Your Own Experiences

If you've ever had your own struggles or experiences with substances, consider sharing them with your teen. Show them that you are human and that you understand temptations.

Discuss Legal Consequences

It's also important to remind them that aside from health risks, there can be legal repercussions. Nothing kills a buzz quite like a criminal record.

All of the above is groundwork, all very important groundwork. But now I want to give you some tips for helping your kid with his refusal skills in the moment:

- **Practice saying no:** Sounds simple, but this is so effective. If he's comfortable saying "no" in various situations, then he'll be more likely to resist temptation in the moment.

- **Teach him to be the designated driver:** This one is a great excuse to avoid drinking and can even make him the hero of the night.

- **Encourage him to take part in the party planning:** If he's organizing the events, he can help to set the tone rather than following it.

- **Remind him that real friends respect boundaries:** If someone can't accept a "no," they're not a true friend.

You are not trying to scare him into acting a certain way. Your goal is to equip him with the knowledge and skills he needs to make informed decisions. We can't be there to hold their hand at every party, but we can make sure they're walking in with their eyes wide open.

Sex and Porn

I bet you're wishing you could go back to those potty training days right now. Hey, if you can handle poonami diaper explosions in the middle of the grocery store, you can handle this. Let's talk about sex, baby. (And porn. Because it's 2024, and that's a thing we have to discuss now.)

Teen Sexuality in the Digital Age

I remember when dating meant holding hands at the movie theater. Now it's all swipe right, slide into DMs, and Netflix and chill. (If you don't know what those mean, ask your teen.)

Online dating and sexting are as common for teens as passing notes was for us. They're playing their own game of romantic ping pong, but instead of a ball, they're batting around heart emojis and eggplant symbols. (If you don't know this one, maybe it's better that way.)

But jokes aside, this digital romance comes with some serious pitfalls:

- **Privacy concerns:** Once something is out there, it's out there. That racy snap might disappear after 10 seconds, but screenshots are forever.

- **Pressure to be "always on:"** Digital connections never sleep, which can lead to unrealistic expectations and burnout.

- **Misunderstandings:** Tone and intent can be hard to read in text, leading to hurt feelings or escalated conflicts.

This is where consent comes in. In the digital age, consent is about more than physical boundaries; it's about digital ones, too. We need to teach our boys that:

- Asking for nudes is not an acceptable "hello."

- Sharing someone's private messages or photos is a big no-no.

- "No" means no, whether it's in person or via text.

Let's not forget about healthy relationships. This world is rife with casual hookups and ghosting, so it's important to also discuss respect, communication, and emotional intimacy. You know, the stuff that makes a relationship more than just a string of fire emojis.

Pornography and its Impact

Thanks to the internet, accessing porn is easier than ordering a pizza. And this stuff can be much more graphic than your father's old Playboy magazine was.

Easy-to-access porn can seriously skew teens' views on sex and relationships. Imagine if you were to try to learn to drive by watching the *Fast and Furious* movies. It's not exactly a recipe for realistic expectations.

Some effects of early exposure to porn can include (Coca & Wikle, 2024):

- unrealistic body expectations (for both themselves and their partners)
- skewed ideas about sexual performance and pleasure
- difficulty forming real, intimate relationships
- potential for addiction (more on that in a bit)

So, how do we address this? First, by acknowledging that curiosity about sex is normal. Then, by having frank discussions about the difference between porn and reality. Some talking points include:

- Porn is a performance, not a how-to guide.
- Real bodies don't look like porn bodies (and that's okay!).
- Consent and communication are key in real-life sexual relationships.
- Love and intimacy are more than just physical acts.

When Does It Become a Problem?

Natural curiosity can cross the line into problematic territory. It's important to know the signs, just in case. These include (Davis, 2022):

- spending excessive time viewing porn to the detriment of other activities
- inability to stop despite wanting to
- escalating to more extreme content over time

- experiencing withdrawal-like symptoms when not engaging with porn

- secrecy and lying about porn use

It's important to note that masturbation is a normal part of teenage sexual development. It becomes a concern only if it's compulsive or interfering with daily life.

When should you seek professional help? If you notice:

- significant changes in behavior or mood related to sexual content

- inability to form real relationships due to porn use

- legal troubles related to sexual behavior (like sexting minors)

- expression of intention to act out sexual fantasies in harmful ways

Shame and punishment have no space here if you really want to help your son through this time in his life. Your goal should be to guide your son toward healthy sexuality and relationships and to help him if he finds himself struggling with any of the above.

Open communication is key, as with everything. Yes, it will be awkward. Yes, you'll both probably want to crawl under a rock at some point. But these conversations are so important for your son's emotional and sexual health.

Practical Tips

I don't blame you if you skipped the chapter and came straight to this section. This one was intense! Kudos if you braved the chapter first. If you didn't, I hope you find time to go back over it all once you feel more confident. Our conditioning makes topics like this really tricky to work through, but with all the work you're putting into parenting, I know you can do this one, too!

Time for your tips:

Work on Open Communication

I've said it before, and I'm going to keep saying it: Create an environment where your son feels safe discussing sensitive topics without fear of judgment.

What NOT to do:

- Don't react with shock or anger when your son shares sensitive information.

- Don't shut down conversations because you feel uncomfortable.

- Don't assume your son knows everything (or nothing) about these topics.

What TO do:

- Remain calm and non-judgmental when discussing sensitive subjects.

- Encourage open dialogue by asking open-ended questions.

- Share age-appropriate personal experiences to build trust.

Educate Yourself and Your Son

Stay informed about the latest trends in teen addiction and share this knowledge with your son.

What Not to do:

- Don't rely solely on outdated information or personal experiences.

- Don't ignore new forms of addiction, such as social media or gaming.

- Don't present information in a preachy or condescending manner.

What TO do:

- Research current trends in teen substance use and behavioral addictions.

- Learn about the science of addiction and share it in an accessible way.

- Encourage critical thinking about addiction and its consequences.

Set Clear Boundaries

Establish rules around screen time, substance use, and online behavior.

What NOT to do:

- Don't set vague or inconsistent rules.

- Don't impose rules without explanation.

- Don't ignore or frequently change established boundaries.

What TO do:

- Clearly communicate your expectations and the reasons behind them.
- Involve your son in setting some of the rules to promote buy-in.
- Consistently enforce boundaries while remaining open to discussion.

Monitor Without Smothering

Keep an eye on your son's behavior while respecting his privacy.

What NOT to do:

- Don't secretly spy on your son's online activities.
- Don't constantly interrogate him about his whereabouts and activities.
- Don't ignore signs of potential addiction because you're afraid to invade privacy.

What TO do:

- Be transparent about any monitoring tools you use.
- Regularly check in with your son about his activities and friends.
- Pay attention to changes in behavior, mood, or social circles.

Promote Healthy Coping Mechanisms

Encourage alternatives to addictive behaviors for managing stress and emotions.

What NOT to do:

- Don't dismiss your son's stress or emotional struggles.
- Don't push activities that don't interest him.
- Don't rely solely on "staying busy" as a prevention strategy.

What TO do:

- Teach and model healthy stress management techniques.
- Encourage involvement in sports, arts, or other engaging activities.
- Discuss the importance of self-care and emotional regulation.

Address Peer Pressure

Equip your son with strategies to handle social situations involving substances or risky behaviors.

What NOT to do:

- Don't underestimate the power of peer influence.
- Don't simply tell him to "just say no."
- Don't assume he'll make the right choice in every situation.

What TO do:

- Role-play potential scenarios to practice refusal skills.
- Discuss the importance of choosing friends who share similar values.
- Offer strategies for exiting uncomfortable situations.

Be Honest About Your Concerns

Share your fears and worries in a constructive manner.

What NOT to do:

- Don't hide your concerns out of fear of pushing your son away.
- Don't express your worries through anger or accusations.
- Don't make your son feel responsible for your emotions.

What TO do:

- Express your concerns calmly and lovingly.
- Explain the reasons behind your worries.
- Emphasize that your concerns come from a place of love and care.

Know When to Seek Help

Recognize the signs that professional intervention might be necessary.

What NOT to do:

- Don't ignore persistent signs of addiction.
- Don't try to handle serious addiction issues on your own.
- Don't delay seeking help out of shame or denial.

What TO do:

- Familiarize yourself with the signs of various addictions.
- Research local resources for teen addiction support.
- Consult with healthcare professionals if you're concerned.

Parenting a teenage boy in today's world is no small feat. There will be days when you feel like you're nailing it and others when you wonder if you're in over your head. That's normal. You're not alone in this journey. There are resources, professionals, and other parents out there who understand what you're going through. Don't hesitate to reach out when you need support or advice.

CHAPTER 6:

Mental Health Matters Know the Signs

Okay, brace yourself for this one: Did you know that 26% of young men in the United States have an anxiety disorder (Mastroianni, 2022)? Yep, that's 1 in 4. And that's just anxiety. We haven't even touched on depression, eating disorders, or other mental health challenges yet.

Now, before you start planning to wrap your son up in bubble wrap and never let him leave the house, take a deep breath. This chapter is not here to scare you. I'm going to help you gain the knowledge and tools to understand and address mental health in your teenage son.

Boys, unfortunately, are the masters of the emotional poker face. They've been told to "man up" and "tough it out" since they were old enough to scrape a knee. As a result, many of our sons are suffering in silence, with their struggles hidden behind a facade of "I'm fine" and the occasional door slam.

In this chapter, we're going to explore why they keep their pain hidden, how to spot the subtle signs that something's not right, and most importantly, how to create an environment where your son feels safe opening up.

Recognizing the signs is only half the battle. The other half is knowing how to respond. With that in mind, we're going to dive into some strategies for supporting your son's mental health as well.

Understanding the Silent Struggles

Have you ever found yourself wondering if your son is just being a typical moody teenager or if there is something more going on? Trust me, we've all been there. Boys often keep their struggles hidden for a variety of reasons (Better Help Editorial Team, 2024; Promises Behavioral Health, 2022):

- **The "man up" mentality:** From a young age, boys are bombarded with messages about what it means to be a man. They're told, "Big boys don't cry" and "Toughen up." Is it any wonder they learn to bottle up their emotions?

- **Fear of judgment:** Vulnerability is often seen as a weakness, so many boys fear being judged or ridiculed for expressing their feelings.

- **Lack of emotional vocabulary:** Sometimes, boys simply don't have the words to express what they're feeling. It's hard to talk about emotions when your go-to descriptors are "fine" and "whatever."

- **Protection instinct:** Believe it or not, some boys hide their pain to protect their parents or friends from worrying. It's like they're carrying the weight of the world on their shoulders.

Society's expectations play a huge role in how boys express (or don't express) their emotions. We live in a culture that often equates masculinity with stoicism and strength. Boys learn early on that showing emotion, particularly sadness or fear, isn't "manly."

This suppression of emotions doesn't just go away. It builds up over time like a pressure cooker without a release valve. When the pressure gets too high, that's when we see explosions of anger, risk-taking behavior, or in some cases, complete emotional shutdown.

Recognizing Subtle Signs of Distress

So if boys are emotional ninjas, hiding their feelings behind masks of "I'm fine," then how are we supposed to know when something's wrong? It's all about becoming attuned to the subtle signs.

Here's what to look out for (*Recognizing the Subtle Signs of Mental Health Challenges*, 2024):

- Changes in behavior:
    - increased irritability or aggression
    - sudden disinterest in activities he used to enjoy
    - risk-taking behavior
- Sleep patterns:
    - difficulty falling asleep
    - sleeping excessively
    - nightmares or night terrors
- Appetite changes:
    - eating much more or less than usual
    - sudden interest in fad diets
- Withdrawal from activities:
    - quitting sports teams or clubs
    - avoiding social gatherings

- Declining academic performance:
    - sudden drop in grades
    - skipping classes
    - lack of motivation for schoolwork
- Shifts in social interaction:
    - withdrawing from friends
    - sudden change in friend groups
    - increased online activity but decreased real-life socializing

One or two of these signs don't automatically mean that there's a problem. You're looking for patterns and significant changes from your son's usual behavior.

The Interplay of Mental Health and Self-Esteem

This is the chicken and egg situation of mental health and self-esteem. Low self-esteem can contribute to mental health issues, and mental health issues can tank self-esteem.

And in today's world of "perfect" social media feeds and highlight reels, it's easier than ever for boys to fall into the comparison trap. They're constantly bombarded with images of "perfect" lives, bodies, and achievements. It's enough to make anyone feel inadequate, let alone a teenager whose sense of self is still developing.

Add to this the pressure to succeed in school, sports, and even their social lives, and you've got a recipe for some serious self-esteem issues. Many boys feel like they're in constant competition, always trying to measure up to impossible standards.

Let's take a look at some strategies for helping to build healthy self-esteem in our boys (*9 Ways to Boost Your Child's Self-Esteem [for Parents]*, 2023):

- **Praise effort, not just results:** Instead of focusing solely on achievements, acknowledge the hard work and perseverance your son puts in.

- **Encourage individuality:** Help your son discover and pursue his own interests, even if they're different from what's "popular."

- **Model self-acceptance:** Show your son that it's okay to be imperfect by accepting your own flaws and mistakes.

- **Teach media literacy:** Help your son understand that what he sees on social media isn't always reality.

- **Provide opportunities for success:** Set your son up with achievable goals to help him build confidence.

- **Validate his feelings:** Show your son that his emotions are valid and important, regardless of what society might say about boys and their feelings.

When Anger Is a Cry for Help

Often, anger and irritability are dismissed as typical teenage behavior, which makes us want to teach them about respect and proper behavior. However, anger can also just be the tip of the iceberg, as we learned earlier. It's the tough guy facade that your son puts on when he's actually feeling vulnerable. Unfortunately, anger can be the socially acceptable mask for a whole range of different emotions that they've been taught not to show.

"Big boys don't cry."

"Man up."

"Don't be a sissy."

With messages like these, is it really any wonder that when they're feeling sad, scared, anxious, worried, or depressed, many boys default to anger?

This is where socialization plays a huge role. Society has long pushed the narrative that "real men" are tough, unemotional, and definitely not vulnerable. So when boys feel emotions that don't fit this mold, they often express them through the one emotion that is seen as "manly"—anger.

So, how do we crack this angry code? We need to look beyond the surface and identify the underlying emotions. Here's a little cheat sheet for you (although this isn't foolproof):

- If the anger comes after a setback or failure, it might be masking feelings of inadequacy or fear of disappointment.
- If it's triggered by social situations, there could be anxiety or insecurity hiding underneath.
- If it's a constant, low-level irritability, it might be a sign of depression.

Start recognizing patterns in your son's angry outbursts. What situations tend to trigger him? Is it always after school? Before big events? When certain topics are brought up?

Let's take an example. Say your son flies off the handle every time you ask about his grades. On the surface, it looks like he's angry about you "nagging" him. But dig a little deeper, and you might find he's actually terrified of disappointing you or anxious about his academic performance.

If you're wondering how you're supposed to react and respond in situations like this, the answer is empathy. It's about connecting with the emotion behind the outburst, not just reacting to the behavior.

Take a look at these techniques for de-escalating angry situations:

- **Stay calm:** I know it's easier said than done when your son is doing his best Hulk impression. But remember, you're the emotional thermostat here. If you stay cool, it'll help him cool down too.

- **Give space:** Sometimes, the best immediate response is no response. Let him know you're there when he's ready to talk, but don't force the issue in the heat of the moment.

- **Validate the feelings, not the behavior:** You might say something like, "I can see you're really upset right now. It's okay to feel angry, but it's not okay to slam doors."

- **Ask, don't tell:** Instead of saying "Calm down!" (which, let's face it, has never calmed anyone down in the history of ever), ask "What's going on?" or "How can I help?"

The tricky part is then encouraging emotional expression beyond anger. Here are some strategies you might use (Lonczak, 2020):

- **Model emotional vocabulary:** Share your own feelings using a wide range of emotional words. "I felt disappointed when..." or "I was anxious about..."

- **Create safe spaces for sharing:** This could be a regular check-in time or even conversations in the car where there's less pressure for eye contact.

- **Praise emotional honesty:** When your son does open up, acknowledge it. "Thank you for sharing that with me. It means a lot that you trust me with your feelings."

- **Use pop culture for discussion:** Discussing the emotions of characters in movies or TV shows can be a less threatening way to explore feelings.

Your son isn't going to turn into an emotional poet overnight, and there will still be slammed doors and grunted responses, but if you can be patient and persistent with these strategies, you can help your son expand his emotional repertoire.

Spotting the Subtle Signs of Self-Harm

This isn't an easy subject, but it's important that we discuss it here. Knowledge is power, and in this case, it could be the power to help your son through a difficult time.

Self-harm isn't about attention-seeking or manipulation. It's a coping mechanism, albeit an unhealthy one, that some teens use to deal with intense emotions or situations they feel they can't control.

Types of self-harm behaviors common in boys include (McKean, 2023):

- cutting or scratching
- burning
- punching walls or hard objects
- head-banging
- interfering with wound healing
- excessive exercise to the point of injury

Boys might engage in self-harm for various reasons (McKean, 2023):

- to release intense emotions they don't know how to express
- to feel a sense of control when everything else feels chaotic
- to punish themselves for perceived failures or flaws
- to feel something when they're feeling numb or disconnected
- to distract from emotional pain by causing physical pain

Boys often choose methods of self-harm that can be explained away as accidents or the result of "rough-housing." This can make detection particularly challenging, so it's important to stay alert for signs.

Less Obvious Indicators

When I say "stay alert," I don't mean to turn you into a paranoid mess. You just need to be aware and observant.

Physical signs to watch out for:

- unexplained cuts, bruises, or burns, especially on arms, legs, or torso
- wearing long sleeves or pants even in warm weather
- frequent "accidents" that result in injuries
- keeping first aid supplies in their room
- patches of missing hair or bald spots

Behavioral changes to be aware of:

- increased desire for privacy beyond the typical teenage need for space
- spending long periods alone in the bathroom or bedroom
- isolation from friends and family
- difficulty handling emotions, with frequent emotional outbursts
- expressing feelings of worthlessness or self-loathing
- keeping sharp objects in easily accessible places

As with everything we've discussed so far in this book, you're looking for a pattern. Again, one or two signs don't necessarily mean your son is self-harming. But if you do notice that pattern emerging, then do take it seriously.

Approaching the Topic Sensitively

If you suspect your son might be self-harming, the way you approach the topic can make all the difference. Here are some tips to help you to express your concern without judgment:

- **Choose the right time and place:** Find a quiet, private moment when you're both calm and not rushed.

- **Start with "I" statements:** "I've noticed..." or "I'm concerned about..." This feels less accusatory than "You're..."

- **Be direct but gentle:** "I've seen some cuts on your arms, and I'm worried you might be hurting yourself. Can we talk about what's going on?"

- **Listen more than you speak:** Give your son space to open up without interrupting or trying to fix things immediately.

- **Avoid reacting with shock or anger:** This can shut down communication and make your son less likely to open up in the future.

- **Offer support, not ultimatums:** "I'm here for you, and we'll get through this together" is more helpful than "You need to stop this right now."

Creating a safe space for open discussion about self-harm is also so important. Here are some tips for doing that:

- **Maintaining a non-judgmental attitude:** Remember, self-harm is a coping mechanism, not a character flaw.

- **Respecting privacy:** Assure your son that you won't share this information unnecessarily.

- **Focusing on feelings, not behaviors:** Ask about what he's feeling that leads to self-harm rather than focusing on the act itself.

- **Being patient:** It may take time for your son to feel comfortable opening up.

- **Offering alternatives:** Discuss healthier ways to cope with difficult emotions.

- **Seeking professional help:** Let your son know that it's okay to need extra support and that you'll help him find it.

I know that discovering that your son is self-harming can be frightening and overwhelming. It's okay to feel scared or upset. Take some time to calm yourself if you need to so that you can then approach the situation with calm and compassion. Your son needs you now more than ever.

Starting the Conversation About Mental Health

This section is the communication hub of our mental health chapter. You've learned to spot the signs; now it's time to talk the talk. I know that starting a conversation with your teenage son might not seem easy, but I'm going to give you some strategies to help get that conversation flowing.

There is no perfect moment to start this conversation. If you're waiting for your son to come to you and say, "Gee, Mom/Dad, I'd love to discuss my emotional well-being," you might be waiting until he's old enough to have teenagers of his own. Sometimes, you just have to take the plunge.

Here are some ways you can initiate the conversation about mental health:

- **The casual approach:** Instead of sitting him down for a formal "talk" (cue the eye rolls), try bringing up the topic during everyday activities. Car rides, while doing chores together, or even during commercial breaks of a show you're watching can be great opportunities.

- **The "I" statements:** Start with your own experiences. "You know, I've been feeling a bit stressed lately. How have you been feeling?" This normalizes the discussion of emotions and mental health.

- **The check in:** Make it a habit to regularly ask, "How are you doing, really?" The key is to ask it in a way that invites more than a one-word answer.

- **The observation:** If you've noticed changes in his behavior, you might say, "I've noticed you seem a bit down lately. Want to talk about it?"

Using current events or media as a conversation starter can be a great way to ease into these discussions, too:

- **News stories:** When mental health issues are in the news, use it as an opening. "I read about this athlete speaking about their depression. What do you think about that?"

- **Movies and TV shows:** Many shows now address mental health. After watching, you could say, "I thought it was interesting how they portrayed anxiety in that character. Have you ever felt anything like that?"

- **Social media:** If your son follows mental health advocates or has shown interest in related content, use that as a springboard. "I noticed you liked that post about stress management. What did you find helpful about it?"

- **Music:** Many artists openly discuss mental health in their lyrics. This can be a great way to connect, especially if it's an artist your son enjoys.

You are not his therapist, and you are not qualified to give him a full-blown therapy session, so don't make that your goal. Instead, focus on just opening the door to these conversations and letting your son know that it's safe and normal to discuss mental health.

Using Active Listening and Validation

You've broken the ice, and your son is talking to you. Now what? This is where we're going to bring active listening back in. It is so important to truly listen to your son. And it's not just about hearing the words he's saying but understanding the feelings behind them. Here are some tips (Cuncic, 2024):

- **Give your full attention:** Put down your phone, turn off the TV, and really focus on what he's saying.

- **Use nonverbal cues:** Nod, maintain appropriate eye contact, and use facial expressions to show that you're engaged.

- **Don't interrupt:** Even if you have the perfect solution or response, hold onto it for a moment. Let him finish his thoughts.

- **Reflect back:** Summarize what you've heard to ensure you've understood correctly. "So what I'm hearing is..."

- **Ask open-ended questions:** Instead of yes-no questions, ask things like, "How did that make you feel?" or "What do you think led to that?"

Next, let's talk about validation. This is where many well-meaning parents stumble. We want to fix things, to make it all better. But sometimes, that's not what our kids need. They need to feel heard and understood. Here's how to validate feelings without minimizing or dismissing them:

- **Acknowledge the emotion:** "It sounds like you're feeling really overwhelmed/anxious/sad."

- **Avoid minimizing:** Phrases like "It's not that bad" or "You'll get over it" can make your son feel like his emotions aren't valid.

- **Don't rush to problem-solve:** Unless your son explicitly asks for solutions, focus on understanding rather than fixing.

- **Normalize the experience:** "It's understandable to feel that way. Many people struggle with similar feelings."

- **Express empathy:** "That sounds really tough. I'm sorry you're going through this."

- **Offer support:** "Thank you for sharing this with me. I'm here for you, whatever you need."

When you can truly listen and validate your son's emotions, you help to create that solid foundation of trust and open communication that will serve you both well. You can't make those feelings go away for him, try as you might. But you can help your son feel safe in expressing them.

Promoting Mental Wellness

Now, I want to take some time here to give you some quick tips for promoting mental wellness in your son's life.

Just like you taught him to brush his teen for dental health, you can also introduce some mental health hygiene practices. Here are some ideas (National Institute of Mental Health, 2024):

- **Physical activity:** Exercise isn't just for six-pack abs (though your son might be more motivated by that). Regular physical activity can be a powerful mood-booster and stress-buster. Encourage him to find a form of exercise he enjoys, whether it's team sports, skateboarding, or even just regular walks.

- **Creative outlets:** Artistic expression can be a great way to process emotions. This could be music, drawing, writing, or even coding. The key is to find something that allows for self-expression.

- **Mindfulness and meditation:** I know, getting a teenage boy to sit still and breathe might seem like a tall order. But even short mindfulness exercises can make a big difference. There are plenty of apps designed for teens that can make this more appealing.

- **Stress-management techniques:** Teach your son practical strategies like deep breathing, progressive muscle relaxation, or even simple time-management skills to help handle stress.

These are all fantastic ways for your son to look after himself, but what can you do to balance being supportive while also allowing him the independence to figure things out for himself?

- **Be available, not intrusive:** Let your son know you're there if he needs you, but respect his need for privacy and autonomy.

- **Encourage problem-solving:** When he comes to you with an issue, resist the urge to jump in with solutions. Instead, ask, "What do you think you could do about that?"

- **Normalize seeking help:** Make it clear that seeking help is a sign of strength, not weakness. Share your own experiences of asking for help when needed.

- **Provide resources:** Make sure your son knows about mental health resources available to him, like school counselors or helplines.

You are the safety net, not the cage. Finding this balance will help your son build the resilience he needs for life's challenges.

Practical Tips

I think we've covered a lot of really useful tips in this chapter. But just in case you came for the CliffsNotes today, here are my practical tips for mental health:

Look Beyond the Surface

Changes in your son's behavior could signal deeper issues.

What NOT to do:

- Don't dismiss mood changes as "just a phase."
- Don't ignore withdrawn behavior or sudden personality shifts.
- Don't assume he'll "grow out of it" without support.

What TO do:

- Notice changes in sleep patterns, appetite, or social interactions.
- Ask open-ended questions to explore his feelings.
- Pay attention to sudden changes in interests or academic performance.

Create a Safe Space for Conversations

Open, judgment-free dialogue is crucial.

What NOT to do:

- Don't react with shock or judgment when he shares.
- Don't interrupt or rush to problem-solve.
- Don't dismiss or minimize his feelings.

What TO do:

- Listen more than you talk.
- Share your own feelings to normalize emotional discussions.
- Validate his emotions, even if you don't understand or agree.

Know the Signs of Self-Harm

Be vigilant but approach with care.

What NOT to do:

- Don't panic or react with anger if you suspect self-harm.
- Don't ignore unexplained injuries or unusual behavior.
- Don't invade privacy without cause, like searching his room.

What TO do:

- Be aware of subtle signs like always wearing long sleeves.
- Approach the topic with concern and empathy, not accusation.

- Seek professional help if you have serious concerns.

Encourage Healthy Coping Mechanisms

Promote positive ways to handle stress.

What NOT to do:

- Don't push activities he's not interested in.
- Don't dismiss the stress he's under.
- Don't rely solely on "toughening up" as a coping strategy.

What TO do:

- Encourage physical activity he enjoys.
- Introduce mindfulness or meditation in small, manageable doses.
- Support creative outlets for emotional expression.

Stay Informed and Involved

Be aware of your son's world.

What NOT to do:

- Don't be oblivious to his online activities.
- Don't dismiss the impact of social media and peer influence.
- Don't avoid difficult topics because they're uncomfortable.

What TO do:

- Stay informed about current teen mental health issues.

- Maintain open discussions about online safety and digital well-being.

- Be involved in his life without being overbearing.

As you close this chapter, I really want you to remember that mental health is not just about addressing problems as they come up but about building resilience, using open communication, and creating an environment where your son feels safe. You're on the front lines of your son's mental health, and that's a big responsibility. But you aren't alone. I'm here. Other parents are here. We've all been through or are going through the same kinds of things. Stay observant, keep the lines of communication open, and don't hesitate to seek professional help when needed.

CHAPTER 7:

Leveling Up— Getting Ready for Adulthood

Your 17-year-old son is standing in front of his bedroom mirror, trying to knot his tie for his first job interview. His hands are shaking, and he's muttering under his breath, "Come on, man up. You can do this." You peek in, wanting to help, but hesitate. Should you step in and fix his tie or let him figure it out on his own?

This chapter is all about that delicate balance: helping your son transition into adulthood while allowing him the space to discover who he truly is. It's about realizing that becoming an adult isn't about conforming to society's checklist or following a prescribed path. It's about your son discovering his authentic self, building confidence from within, and finding the courage to chart his own course.

We're going to explore that transition of late adolescence into adulthood and discuss how to help him break free from the restrictive "be a man" mentality, build genuine self-esteem, and find his purpose and passion.

If you need to take a moment here to look at his baby pictures, go ahead. I'll be ready when you are.

The Journey to Adulthood

One minute, your son is excited about the future, ready to take on the world, and the next, he's hiding under his covers, wishing he could stay a kid forever.

This period of his life is full of many conflicting emotions:

- excitement about newfound freedoms and opportunities
- anxiety about increased responsibilities and expectations
- pride in growing independence
- fear of the unknown future
- eagerness to prove oneself
- insecurity about one's abilities

It's a lot, especially for a teenager whose brain is still under construction. Let's also take a look at some of the common challenges that boys will face during this transition:

- **Identity crisis:** "Who am I, really?" becomes the question of the hour (and day, and year).
- **Decision paralysis:** Suddenly, every choice feels monumental. What if I choose the wrong college/career/girlfriend?
- **Impostor syndrome:** Many boys feel like they're just pretending to be adults, waiting for someone to call their bluff.
- **Financial fears:** The realization that money doesn't, in fact, grow on trees can be a rude awakening.
- **Social shifts:** Friendships change, romantic relationships get more serious, and family dynamics evolve.
- **Skill gaps:** Realizing there's a lot they don't know how to do yet (hello, laundry and taxes).

This is where you come in, parents. Your job is to help your son see change not as a terrifying monster under the bed but as an exciting opportunity for growth. Easier said than done, right?

If your son is struggling with anxiety about the future, firstly, remind him that this is normal. The unknown can be scary, but you can help him work through it. Help him break big, overwhelming goals into smaller, manageable steps.

Sometimes, facing our fears head-on can make them less scary. Ask him, "What's the worst that could happen?" Then, you can help him problem-solve from there. You can also teach your son mindful techniques to stay present rather than getting lost in those future worries.

Finally, it's important that he knows mistakes are normal and that you'll be there to support him if things don't go as planned.

Supporting Self-Discovery

This can be a bit of a wild ride—exciting and scary all at once! Your son is a bit like a scientist during this stage, constantly experimenting with different identities and roles. One day, he might be the budding philosopher, chatting about the meaning of life over his bowl of cereal. The next, he's decided that he's going to be the next big thing in underground rap. You can think of yourself as his supporting (and sometimes bemused) lab assistant.

What if his experiments involve green hair? Or he develops a passion for extreme ironing? (Yes, that's a real thing. Look it up if you need a chuckle.)

Well, unless his experiments are harmful, you should try to stay open and curious. Today's "ridiculous" phase might be tomorrow's successful career. After all, who would have thought that playing video games could become a million-dollar profession? Think of the YouTube views if he took up extreme ironing or something like that.

It's actually a really good thing for your son to expose himself to as many diverse experiences as possible. It's like taking him to an all-you-can-eat buffet of life experiences. The more he tries, the more likely he is to find something that really resonates with him. So, encourage him to join that pottery class, try out for the school play, or volunteer at the local animal shelter. Who knows? You might be raising the next great ceramicist, actor, or zoologist.

As he's exploring, be his personal interviewer. Ask open-ended questions like, "What did you enjoy about that?" or "How did that make you feel?" These questions aren't just to satisfy your parental curiosity (though that's a nice bonus). They're to help him reflect on his experiences and understand himself better.

The tricky part for you might be making sure you are still that safe space for all this experimentation. Think of your home as a judgment-free zone, like a yoga class, but with fewer downward dogs and more teenage angst. Make it clear that your love and support are unconditional, whether he wants to be a corporate lawyer or a professional juggler.

Remember to respect his privacy, too. Yes, I know it's tempting to "accidentally" overhear his phone conversations or sneak a peek at his journal. But unless you have serious concerns, resist the urge. Trust me, he'll appreciate the space and be more likely to open up to you voluntarily.

Speaking of opening up, sometimes your son just needs to talk things out. So, be a sounding board. Listen more than you speak. And I mean really listen, not just waiting for your turn to impart your infinite parental wisdom.

Lastly, model self-acceptance. Show him that it's okay to be imperfect, to change your mind, to not have all the answers. Share stories about your own journey of self-discovery (yes, even that phase where you thought mullets were cool).

Breaking Free From the "Be a Man" Mentality

Here, you're going to be taking a wrecking ball to some age-old stereotypes, particularly those pesky "be a man" messages that society keeps hammering into our boys' heads.

Let's start with a little game. I'll list some common phrases, and you count how many times you've heard them (or, gulp, said them yourself):

- "Man up!"
- "Boys don't cry."
- "Don't be such a girl."
- "Tough it out."
- "Real men don't show fear."

How many did you get? If you're like most people, you've probably lost count. These phrases are so ingrained in our culture that they're practically background noise. But here's the thing: This "background noise" is actually a loud, harmful message that's messing with our boys' heads.

These stereotypes tell our sons that to be a "real man," they need to be tough, unemotional, always in control, and never, ever vulnerable. It's like we're asking them to be some kind of emotional Terminator. And let me tell you, that's a heavy burden for anyone to carry, let alone a young man still figuring himself out.

The impact of that is like giving our boys emotional straight jackets. They start bottling up their feelings, afraid to express themselves or ask for help. This can lead to all sorts of issues, from anxiety and depression to aggressive behavior and difficulty forming genuine connections. In short, we're setting them up for a lifetime of emotional constipation. It's not a pretty picture, is it?

Redefining Masculinity

So, if we're tearing down these old ideas of what it means to "be a man," what are we building in their place? Well, how about we start with the radical notion that there's no one "right" way to be a man?

Imagine masculinity not as a narrow path but as a vast, open field. In this field, there's room for the sports-loving, car-fixing stereotypical "guy's guy." But there's also space for the sensitive poet, the nurturing caregiver, the fashion-loving stylist, and everything in between. Heck, your son could be all of these things and more!

The key is to encourage your son to explore and embrace all facets of his personality. Teach him that strength isn't about suppressing emotions but about having the courage to feel them and express them. Real bravery is not about never being afraid; it's about feeling the fear and doing it anyway.

Finally, let's talk about emotional intelligence and vulnerability here, too. These are superpowers in disguise, and I know we've touched on these already in the book, but they are so relevant here. A man who can understand and manage his own emotions, who can empathize with others, and who isn't afraid to be vulnerable is a man who is going to have healthier relationships, better mental health, and probably a more successful career, too. That's a secret weapon he can keep for life.

Challenging Toxic Messages

This all sounds great, right? But how do we help our sons stand up to all these toxic messages out there?

Well, I'm glad you asked!

First, we need to teach our sons to be critical thinkers. The next time you're watching a movie or TV show together, play a little game I like to call "Spot the Stereotype." Pause the show and ask your son, "What do you think about how they're portraying men here? Does this seem realistic to you?" Get him to flex those critical thinking muscles.

Encourage your son to question everything. When he hears someone say, "That's not what guys do," teach him to ask, "Says who?" Help him understand that these societal messages aren't laws of nature—they're just ideas, and often outdated ones at that.

The real work for you is this, though: You have to walk the walk. If you want your son to challenge these stereotypes, you need to be doing it too. Moms, show him how you stand up to stereotypes and advocate for all expressions of self. Dads, share times when you've felt pressured to "man up." Talk about how you deal with emotions. Cry at sappy movies together! Show him that it's okay for men to have a full range of emotions.

Supporting your son in standing up against harmful stereotypes isn't always easy. He might face pushback from peers or even other adults. But remind him that every time he challenges these toxic ideas, he's not just helping himself—he's making the world a little bit better for everyone.

Building Self-Esteem From the Inside Out

Now, let's talk about how you can help your son build his self-esteem. There are many things that contribute to healthy self-esteem, but we'll start with working on his self-compassion.

Working on Self-Compassion

We need to teach our boys to be their own best friends. Sounds simple enough, except that the world is regularly telling them to be tough on themselves, so it's actually a bit like swimming against the tide.

Imagine your son has just bombed a math test. His inner voice might be saying something like, "You're so stupid. You'll never be good at this." Ouch, right? That's where self-compassion comes in. We want to replace that harsh inner critic with a kinder, more understanding voice.

Try teaching your son to talk to himself as he would to a good friend. Would he call his buddy "stupid" for failing a test? Probably not. He'd likely say something like, "Hey, that test was really tough. But you studied hard, and I bet you'll do better next time." That's the kind of self-talk we're aiming for.

I do have a simple trick for this one, too: Encourage your son to use his own name when practicing self-talk. So instead of "I can do this," try "Tom, you can do this." It might sound a bit weird at first, but research shows it can be more effective (Bergland, 2017). It's like he's getting a pep talk from his very own personal coach!

And remember, self-compassion isn't about making excuses or avoiding responsibility. It's about treating ourselves with kindness and understanding, even when we mess up. Because let's face it, we all mess up sometimes. It's part of being human.

Recognizing Personal Strengths

Next up, you're going to help your son recognize his personal strengths. No, you're not going to turn him into an egomaniac who thinks he's God's gift to the world by doing this. You're simply helping him to see and appreciate his unique qualities.

It's really easy for boys to lose sight of their individual strengths in this world that's obsessed with likes, followers, and standardized test scores. Maybe your son isn't a straight-A student or the star quarterback, but he has a knack for making people laugh, or he's great at resolving conflicts among his friends. These are valuable strengths that deserve recognition!

Try this: At dinner each night, ask everyone to share one thing they did well that day. It doesn't have to be anything big. Maybe your son helped a classmate understand a tough concept, or he finally mastered that tricky guitar chord he's been practicing. The point is to get him in the habit of recognizing his own strengths and accomplishments.

Let's try to move beyond societal measures of success. Sure, good grades and athletic achievements are great. But what about kindness?

Creativity? Resilience? These qualities are just as important (if not more so) in the grand scheme of life. Help your son see that success comes in many forms and that his unique blend of qualities is something to be celebrated.

Celebrating Growth and Effort

Last but definitely not least, let's talk about the power of celebrating growth and effort. In other words, it's time to channel your inner sports commentator and get excited about the process, not just the outcome!

When we're watching a sports match, we don't just cheer when our team scores a goal. We cheer for great passes, clever strategies, and players picking themselves up after a fall. Life should be the same way. Did your son study hard for a test, even if he didn't ace it? That's worth celebrating. Did he step out of his comfort zone and try something new? Break out the party hats!

This approach is all about fostering a growth mindset. It's the belief that our abilities and intelligence can be developed through effort, good strategies, and help from others. It's the difference between "I'm not good at this" and "I'm not good at this *yet*."

A fun way to reinforce this is to create a family "Effort Wall." Whenever someone in the family puts in a solid effort towards a goal, write it on a sticky note and add it to the wall. By the end of the month, you'll have a visual representation of all the hard work and growth that's happened.

What I want you to take away from this section is that building self-esteem isn't about showering our kids with empty praise. It's about helping them develop a deep, unshakable sense of their own worth. It's about equipping them with the tools to pick themselves up when they fall, to recognize their own value, and to keep growing and learning throughout their lives.

Encouraging Independence and Self-Reliance

It's time for some tough love. Not for your son, but for you. We're about to enter the parental twilight zone known as "letting go." Don't panic! I promise it's not as scary as it sounds. In fact, it can be pretty exciting if you approach it right.

Balancing Support and Freedom

Do you remember when you taught your son to ride a bike? At first, you were running alongside, holding the seat. But at some point, you had to let go and watch him wobble off on his own. Encouraging independence is a lot like that, except the bike is life, and the wobbling never really stops (as I'm sure we all know!).

Our job is to find the sweet spot between helicopter parenting and a completely hands-off approach. We're being that safety net for him again here.

You can start by giving your son more control over his daily life decisions. Let him choose his own clothes (even if that means he goes to school looking like he got dressed in the dark), manage his homework schedule, or decide how to spend his allowance (yes, even if he blows it all on candy!).

When he comes to you with a problem, you should resist the urge to swoop in with a solution. Instead, try asking, "What do you think you should do?" You'll be amazed at how often he'll come up with a good solution on his own. And if he doesn't... Well, that's a learning opportunity right there.

Be available for advice, but let him take the lead. Be his Yoda—dispense wisdom, you must, but fight his battles, you must not.

Teaching Life Skills

Being an adult is a lot easier if you go into it knowing how. I'm talking about the practical skills we need; I know I'm not alone in wondering at what point in life you actually feel like a grown-up.

So start with the basics: doing laundry without turning everything pink, cooking a few simple meals that aren't just ramen, and managing a budget because hoping for the best is not a financial strategy.

But don't stop there! Teach him how to change a tire, how to sew a button, and how to write a professional email. These might seem like small things, but they add up to a young man who can handle whatever life throws at him.

You can also encourage problem-solving and resourcefulness. The next time something breaks in the house, involve him in fixing it. If he can't figure it out, great! Then, it's time to learn how to research solutions, read instructions, or know when to call in an expert.

The goal is to help him find his "I can figure this out" attitude. As you well know, in the adult world, there is no instruction manual. There is Google now, but knowing how to use it effectively is half the battle.

Using Failure as a Learning Opportunity

Let's talk about the F-word. Failure. Not the other F-word. Let's see if we can reframe this to reflect what it really is: a fantastic learning opportunity.

Your son is going to fail. Multiple times. In big ways and small ways. And that's not just okay; it's great! Each failure is a chance to learn and grow more resilient.

The next time he does fail, don't try to fix it or brush it off with a "better luck next time." Instead, help him to analyze what happened. What went wrong? What could he do differently next time?

Teach him to see mistakes not as endpoints but as stepping stones. Did he bomb the presentation? Great, now he knows he needs to prepare more thoroughly. Did he forget to set an alarm and oversleep? Fantastic, he's learned the importance of time management (and maybe investing in a louder alarm clock).

You can also share your own failure stories with him. Yes, even the embarrassing ones. Doing this shows him that everyone messes up sometimes and that it's not the failure that defines you—it's how you respond to it.

Realistically, your son isn't going to have a failure-free life. So, teach him how to bounce back when things do go wrong.

Finding Purpose and Passion

First off, don't panic if your son's current passion seems to be perfecting his gaming skills or gathering the perfect meme collection. We're going to explore how to help him uncover the deeper stuff that really lights his fire.

This isn't about deciding on a career path (though that might come later). It's about uncovering his core values and interests. You can start by simply encouraging him to try new things. And I mean really try new things. If he's always been a sports guy, maybe suggest he give theater a shot. If he's more of an indoor kid, how about some wilderness survival skills? The idea is to expose him to a buffet of experiences. Who knows? He might discover he has a hidden talent for underwater basket weaving or a passion for competitive dog grooming. (Hey, stranger things have happened!)

A fun exercise for this is the "What If" game. Ask him questions like, "What would you do if money wasn't an issue?" or "If you could solve one problem in the world, what would it be?" His answers can provide valuable insights into what truly matters to him.

You're not trying to push him toward any particular interest or value but helping him try to uncover what really matters to him. Once he knows that really matters to him, you can help him connect those passions to his future. Now, I am not saying you need to map out his entire life here (most of us are still figuring this out well into our 40s). You can help him see how his passions can shape his future in meaningful ways.

You start by broadening his view of what a "successful" future looks like. Sure, a high-paying job and a nice car are great, but what about personal fulfillment? Making a difference in the world? Work–life balance? Help him see that there are many paths to a rewarding life.

Encourage him to explore how his interests could translate into various career paths. Does he love gaming? That could lead to careers in game design, e-sports management, or even using gamification in education or business. Is he passionate about the environment? That could lead to careers in sustainable design, environmental law, or green energy technology.

But remember that purpose isn't just about career. You can also help your son see how his passions can contribute to his community or make the world a better place. Maybe his love of dogs could lead him to volunteer at an animal shelter. Or his coding skills could be used to create an app that helps elderly neighbors connect with local services.

The key is to help him see that his interests and skills have value beyond just personal enjoyment or academic achievement. They're tools he can use to craft a meaningful, purposeful life.

And here's a final thought: Remind your son (and yourself) that finding one's purpose isn't a one-time event. It's a lifelong journey of exploration, adjustment, and growth. The goal isn't to have it all figured out by 18 or 21 or even 41. It's to build a curiosity about life, a willingness to try new things, and the resilience to keep going even when the path isn't clear.

Practical Tips

What a wholesome chapter, if I do say so myself! We've covered a lot of useful strategies, but in case you need a quick reference, this practical tip section is your best friend:

Encourage Self Exploration

Your son's journey to adulthood is like a grand adventure, and you're his trusty sidekick.

What NOT to do:

- Don't push your own unfulfilled dreams onto him.
- Don't dismiss interests that seem impractical or temporary.
- Don't limit his experiences to what's familiar or comfortable.

What TO do:

- Support him in trying new activities, even if they seem out of character.
- Ask open-ended questions about his experiences and feelings.
- Provide resources and opportunities to explore diverse interests.

Challenge Stereotypes About Manhood

It's time to rewrite the "man code."

What **NOT** to do:

- Don't reinforce harmful phrases like "man up" or "boys don't cry."

- Don't criticize behaviors or interests for being "unmanly."

- Don't equate vulnerability with weakness.

What **TO** do:

- Encourage emotional expression and authenticity.

- Discuss and challenge societal stereotypes about masculinity.

- Model healthy emotional expression yourself.

Promote Independence With Guidance

Think of yourself as a GPS, not a driver.

What **NOT** to do:

- Don't solve all his problems for him.

- Don't micromanage his daily life.

- Don't shield him from all potential failures.

What TO do:

- Give him space to make decisions and learn from mistakes.
- Offer guidance and support when asked.
- Teach essential life skills for adulthood.

Celebrate Effort, Not Just Achievement

Life's a journey, not just a destination.

What NOT to do:

- Don't focus solely on grades, trophies, or other external measures of success.
- Don't compare his achievements to others.
- Don't dismiss the value of trying and failing.

What TO do:

- Praise his effort, growth, and resilience.
- Acknowledge the learning process, not just the outcome.
- Help him set and work towards personal goals.

Model Positive Self-Esteem

Be the change you want to see.

What NOT to do:

- Don't engage in negative self-talk in front of your son.

- Don't base your self-worth solely on achievements or appearance.

- Don't shy away from admitting your own mistakes and growth.

What TO do:

- Demonstrate healthy self-esteem in your own life.

- Share your own experiences of personal growth and learning.

- Show that it's okay to be imperfect and to keep evolving.

There is no one-size-fits-all approach to becoming a man. Your son's path will be as unique as he is. You're already giving him the best possible foundation for adulthood by being here and learning all these things with me. Take a deep breath and trust in your son's journey and in your ability to support him along the way.

CHAPTER 8:

"Parents Aren't Perfect" A Teen's Guide to You

You're rummaging through old photos and come across one of you and your son from just a few years ago. In the photo, you're beaming as you help him with his science project. Fast forward to today, and you find yourself staring at a closed bedroom door, wondering when your little scientist turned into this grunting, eye-rolling creature who seems to think you're from another planet.

If this scenario hits a little too close to home, welcome to the club! You're not alone in feeling like you've somehow stumbled into an alternate universe where everything you thought you knew about parenting has been turned on its head.

This chapter is going to explore parent evolution. We'll learn how to see ourselves through our teens' eyes, how to break down the barriers that seem to spring up overnight, and how to adapt our parenting style to meet the needs of our changing sons.

This journey isn't just about understanding our teens better. It's about understanding ourselves better, too. As we help our sons figure out who they are, we're redefining our own roles and identities in the process. It's a two-way street of growth and change, and understanding each other better is the key to getting through it together.

Seeing Ourselves Through Their Eyes

Let's start with a little exercise: I want you to imagine you're your teenage son for a moment. (No, you don't have to start speaking in monosyllables or develop a sudden aversion to showers.) Now, think about how you—the parent—might appear through his eyes.

If you're picturing a nagging, overbearing killjoy who's perpetually out of touch with reality, congratulations! You've just tapped into some common teen perceptions of parents. Here are a few greatest hits from the "My Parents Just Don't Get It" album:

- **The Overbearing Helicopter:** Always hovering, never giving any space.

- **The Critic-in-Chief:** Nothing is ever good enough.

- **The Out-of-Touch Fossil:** Hopelessly clueless about anything remotely current.

- **The Hypocrite:** "Do as I say, not as I do."

- **The Warden:** Rules, rules, and more rules.

Now, before you start feeling like the world's worst parent, remember: These perceptions aren't necessarily accurate. They're more like funhouse mirror reflections—distorted versions of reality.

So why do teens often see us this way? Well, part of it is the natural push for independence. As they strive to establish their own identities, teens often define themselves in opposition to their parents. It's like they're playing a game of "Opposite Day" that lasts for years.

Another factor is their developing brain. The teenage brain is wired to seek novelty and take risks, which can make our cautious, responsible adult behavior seem boring or restrictive. Plus, their ability to see things from others' perspectives is still developing, which can make it hard for them to understand our motivations.

Separating Perception From Reality

While these teen perceptions might make us want to pull our hair out, it's important to remember that they're not an accurate reflection of who we are as parents or people. You see, just as we're not actually the fun-sucking dictators they sometimes make us out to be, our teens aren't the ungrateful, lazy slobs we might be tempted to label them as in our moments of frustration. The truth, as always, lies somewhere in the middle.

Our teens' perceptions of us are heavily influenced by their own developmental stage. They are in the middle of a major identity overhaul, trying to figure out who they are and where they fit in the world. This process often involves pushing against the boundaries we set and the values we represent, not because they necessarily disagree with them, but because they need to question everything to figure out what they truly believe.

Bridging that perception gap involves using our old friend empathy again. We need to put ourselves in our teen's shoes and try to see the world from their perspective. My advice here is the same as every time we've discussed empathy: listen more and talk less, ask questions, validate their feelings, share your own experiences, and admit when you're wrong.

You are not here to be your teen's best friend or to agree with everything they say and do. You are responsible for creating a foundation of mutual understanding and respect.

Breaking Down the Barriers

It's really common for emotional and communication barriers to develop during adolescence. Let's see if we can do some major demolition work on those walls, shall we? Don't worry; we won't talk about actual property damage, even though I know some days you might be tempted.

Let's start by identifying the usual suspects in the line-up of parent–teen barriers:

- **Communication breakdowns:** Do you remember when your teen used to chatter non-stop about everything? Now, getting more than a grunt or an eye roll feels like pulling teeth. It's like someone replaced your chatty kid with a surly caveman overnight.

- **Emotional distance:** There was a time when a hug from you could solve all problems. Now, your teen acts like you have the plague if you so much as pat their shoulder in public.

- **Trust issues:** Whether it's because of broken promises, invasion of privacy, or just the natural skepticism of adolescence, trust can become a rare commodity in the parent–teen relationship.

These barriers don't pop up because you're a bad parent or because your teen is trying to make your life miserable (even though it might feel that way sometimes). They're often a natural part of the adolescent push for independence. But natural doesn't mean inevitable or insurmountable. Let's take a look at some strategies for chipping away at these walls.

Initiating Open and Honest Conversations

It starts with open and honest communication. Here are some quick tips to get the ball rolling:

- **Choose your moment:** Trying to have a deep conversation when your teen is hangry, tired, or in the middle of a Fortnite battle is a recipe for disaster. Look for calm, relaxed moments.

- **Use "I" statements:** Instead of "You never talk to me," try "I miss our conversations and would love to hear about your day."

- **Ask open-ended questions:** "How was school?" will likely get you a one-word answer. "What was the most interesting thing that happened today?" might get you a bit more.

- **Create a judgment-free zone:** Make it clear that they can share without fear of immediate consequences or lectures. Sometimes, they just need to be heard.

Showing Parental Vulnerability

What if parents admitted that we don't have all the answers? I know it's a shocking idea, but hear me out.

Showing vulnerability by sharing our own struggles, admitting our mistakes, and expressing our fears can be incredibly powerful when connecting with our teens. It shows them that it's okay to be imperfect and that emotions are normal and can be expressed safely. It also shows them that we trust and respect them enough to be real with them.

Try sharing stories from your own teenage years, including the mistakes and the lessons learned. Talk about your current challenges and how you're dealing with them. Let them see that adulting is a continuous journey of growth and learning, not a destination you magically arrive at when you turn 18.

This openness can bridge the gap with teens, showing them that you're not just an authority figure but a real person they can relate to and trust. It's like extending a hand across the divide, inviting connection rather than enforcing separation.

Adapting Your Parenting Style

Maybe it's time for a wardrobe change? I want you to try on some new parenting styles with me. They might feel a little uncomfortable at first, but like a good pair of jeans, they'll soften up with wear.

From Director to Mentor

When your kid was little, you were the all-knowing, all-powerful director of the show called *Their Life*. Now, it's time for a role change.

As your teen grows, you need to transition from the director yelling "Action!" and "Cut!" to more of a behind-the-scenes mentor.

This means shifting from a rule-based approach to a more collaborative one. Instead of laying down the law, try involving your teen in setting guidelines. Ask for their input on family rules and expectations. You might be surprised at how reasonable they can be (sometimes).

The tricky part is balancing guidance with their increasing need for autonomy. It's a bit like teaching them to ride a bike all over again, but this time, the bike is life, and you can't hold onto the seat forever. You need to let them pedal on their own but stay close enough to catch them if they wobble.

Setting Boundaries While Encouraging Independence

Before you jump to conclusions: Do not turn your home into a teen-ruled anarchy where they can do whatever they want. Instead, adapt your style; don't abdicate your role. The key is to maintain your authority while allowing room for growth.

Try negotiating boundaries together. For example, instead of setting a rigid curfew, discuss what a reasonable time might be and why. Explain your concerns (safety, adequate sleep) and listen to their perspective. You might agree on a trial period for a new curfew time, with the understanding that it will be reviewed based on how well they handle the responsibility.

This approach does two things: It shows respect for their growing maturity, and it teaches valuable skills in negotiation and responsibility. Plus, when teens have a say in setting rules, they're more likely to follow them. (No guarantees, but hey, it's worth a shot!)

Supporting Without Controlling

So, how do you offer support without turning into a helicopter parent? How do you help without taking over?

Be a safety net, not a cage.

Let your teen know you're there if they need you, but resist the urge to swoop in and fix everything. When they come to you with a problem, instead of immediately offering solutions, try asking, "What do you think you should do?" Help them walk through the problem-solving process.

Encourage them to take age-appropriate risks and learn from their mistakes. Did they forget to study for a test? As much as it pains you, let them face the consequences. Then, help them figure out how to do better next time.

This approach might feel uncomfortable at first. Watching our kids struggle or fail goes against every parental instinct we have. But remember, your goal isn't to raise a perfect teen; it's to raise a capable adult. And capability comes from experience—both successes and failures.

Show your teen that you trust them to grow and learn, and this will help them gain the skills and confidence to face the big wide world. It will also strengthen your relationship with them.

Connecting Through Their World

Have you thought about immersing yourself in teen culture as a parenting strategy? I can already picture a sea of horrified faces staring at this page. Don't worry, I promise it's not as scary as it seems. You might even find it... dare I say... fun?

Show Genuine Interest

Showing interest in your teen's world doesn't mean you need to start wearing baggy jeans or pepper your conversation with "yeet" and "sus." (Please, for the love of all that is holy, don't do that.) It's about engaging with their interests in a genuine, non-intrusive way.

Start by asking questions about the things they enjoy. What's their favorite game? Who's their favorite YouTuber? Why do they like that particular music artist? The key here is to listen without judgment. Yes, even if you think their music sounds like a cat caught in a blender. Remember, the goal is connection, not critique.

Try saying something like, "I noticed you really enjoy [insert interest here]. What do you like about it?" Then, actually listen to their answer. You might be surprised at the depth of thought behind their interests.

Bridging the Generational Gap

It might seem like your teen is speaking a foreign language half the time (what in the world is a "finsta"?), but with a little effort, you can start to understand their world.

One strategy is to ask your teen to be your cultural guide. Let them introduce you to their favorite shows, music, or games. Yes, it might mean sitting through a few TikTok compilations, but hey, that's a small price to pay for connection.

Another approach is to find common ground in your experiences. Sure, the technology might be different, but the emotions are often the same. Did you ever feel misunderstood by your parents? Struggle with friend drama? Share these experiences. It shows your teen that while the details might be different, the core experiences of growing up are universal.

Participating in Their Lives

Participating in your teen's life is a delicate balance. You want to be involved but not overbearing. Interested, but not intrusive. It feels impossible sometimes, I know!

Look for organic ways to participate. If they're into sports, offer to kick a ball around with them. If they love cooking videos, suggest trying out a recipe together. The key is to offer, not impose. Let them take the lead.

And remember, respecting their privacy is crucial. Knock before entering their room. Ask before posting about them on social media. Show them that you respect their boundaries, and they'll be more likely to invite you into their world.

The Need for Parental Self-Reflection

As much as this journey is about understanding our teens, it's also about understanding ourselves. Parenting is a journey filled with joy, challenges, and continuous learning. It is easy to become consumed with day-to-day responsibilities, leaving little time for introspection.

Self-reflection isn't new, and it's not mumbo jumbo, either. It's a powerful tool that can significantly benefit your relationship with your teen. When we can understand our own thoughts, feelings, and reactions, we can respond to our teens more effectively and compassionately (Martelo, 2023).

Try this: The next time you have a conflict with your teen, take a moment to ask yourself, "Why am I reacting this way? What's really bothering me here?" You might be surprised at what you discover. Maybe their behavior reminds you of something you struggled with, or perhaps it's triggering a fear you have about their future.

One effective technique for self-reflection is journaling. Don't worry, you don't need to write a novel. Even a few minutes of jotting down your thoughts can provide valuable insights.

Recognizing Parental Influence

I'm going to tell you something that might shock you now: A lot of your teen's behavior is a reflection of you. Scary, right? As parents, we're our kids' first and most influential role models.

This means that our behavior has a huge impact on our teens, whether we realize it or not. If we want our teens to be open and communicative, we need to model that behavior. If we want them to handle stress well, we need to demonstrate healthy stress management ourselves.

Take a moment to think about the messages you're sending through your actions. Are you practicing what you preach? If not, don't beat yourself up. Remember, you're human too. The important thing is to recognize areas where you can improve and make an effort to do so.

Adapting to Changing Needs

One of the trickiest parts of parenting a teen is that their needs are constantly evolving. What worked last year, or even last month, might not work now. This is where ongoing self-reflection becomes crucial.

You should regularly check in with yourself about your parenting approach. Is it still effective? Is it meeting your teen's current needs? Don't be afraid to adjust your strategies as your teen grows and changes.

Adapting doesn't mean you're being inconsistent. It means you're flexible and responsive to your teen's development. It shows that you're growing alongside them.

Here's a strategy for continuous growth: Set aside time each month for a parenting check-in. Reflect on what's working well and what could use some tweaking. Consider asking your teen for feedback, too. You might be surprised at their insights.

In the end, remember that perfect parenting doesn't exist. What does exist is thoughtful, adaptive, reflective parenting. It's about being willing to learn, grow, and change along with your teen. It's about showing up, day after day, even when it's hard. And trust me, that's more than enough.

Practical Tips

Here's your cheat sheet for evolving parenthood:

See Through Their Eyes

Try to understand your teen's perspective, even when it differs from yours.

What NOT to do:

- Don't dismiss their feelings as "just a phase."
- Don't assume you know exactly what they're thinking or feeling.
- Don't take their criticisms or mood swings personally.

What TO do:

- Listen more than you speak.
- Ask open-ended questions to understand their viewpoint.
- Acknowledge their feelings, even if you disagree with their actions.

Break Down Barriers

Work on improving communication and emotional connection.

What NOT to do:

- Don't force conversations when they're not ready.
- Don't react with anger or disappointment when they open up.
- Don't invade their privacy in an attempt to stay connected.

What TO do:

- Create regular, low-pressure opportunities for conversation.
- Share appropriate personal experiences to show vulnerability.
- Respect their need for privacy while maintaining open lines of communication.

Adapt Your Parenting Style

Evolve your approach as your teen grows.

What NOT to do:

- Don't cling to rules or methods that no longer fit their age or maturity level.
- Don't give up all structure in an attempt to be their "friend."
- Don't expect them to handle adult responsibilities without guidance.

What TO do:

- Involve them in setting rules and consequences.

- Gradually increase their autonomy as they demonstrate responsibility.

- Offer guidance and support without taking over their problems.

Connect Through Their World

Show genuine interest in their interests and culture.

What NOT to do:

- Don't mock or belittle their interests, even if you don't understand them.

- Don't try too hard to be "cool" or use their slang inappropriately.

- Don't force your way into their social circles or online spaces.

What TO do:

- Ask questions about their interests and listen without judgment.

- Let them introduce you to their music, shows, or games.

- Respect their social boundaries while showing you're available and interested.

Practice Self-Reflection

Continuously examine and improve your own parenting.

What NOT to do:

- Don't assume your parenting doesn't need to change as your teen grows.

- Don't ignore your own emotional reactions and triggers.

- Don't expect perfection from yourself (or your teen).

What TO do:

- Regularly assess what's working and what isn't in your parenting approach.

- Be willing to apologize and make changes when you make mistakes.

- Model the self-awareness and growth you want to see in your teen.

Parenting a teenager isn't about having all the answers or never making mistakes. It's about being willing to learn, adapt, and grow alongside our kids. It's a journey of mutual growth and understanding. There will be bumps along the way, moments of frustration, and times when you feel like you're speaking different languages. But there will also be moments of connection, laughter, and love that make it all worthwhile.

Bonus Chapter: Parenting Hacks

Let's begin with a story: 15-year-old Martin slouches into the kitchen with his headphones on and wearing a classic teen scowl on his face. His mom, Maeve, is about to launch into the usual "How was your day?" that typically gets a grunt in response. But instead, she remembers a tip from her parenting group. She casually mentions, "Hey, I heard that new song you like on the radio today. It's pretty catchy."

Martin pauses and takes off his headphones. For the next 10 minutes, they have an amazing conversation—probably the best they've had in weeks—all about music.

This is the power of parenting hacks, where small actions can make a big difference in your relationship with your teen. This bonus chapter is all about those little strategies, those seemingly insignificant moves that can yield surprising results in connecting with your adolescent enigma.

Think of these as your parenting cheat codes. They're simple, effective strategies you can start using right away to build a stronger bond with your teen. We're talking quick wins here—no need for grand gestures or major life overhauls.

Now, I might sound like a broken record here, but the real power is in consistency. It's not about making one big effort and expecting miracles. It's about consistently making small efforts, day in and day out. It's the parenting equivalent of compound interest—those little deposits of attention, understanding, and positive reinforcement add up over time to create a rich, trusting relationship with your teen.

Building Confidence

I want to start with confidence. In this world, a teen's self-esteem can rise and fall as quickly as you can blink, so the trick is to help them build genuine, lasting confidence. But don't worry, you don't need a radioactive spider or a secret government program to do it. Just a few simple, consistent strategies can make a world of difference.

Celebrating Small Wins

First, become your teen's personal cheerleader (minus the pom-poms, unless you really want to embarrass them). The key here is to regularly acknowledge their efforts, no matter how small. Did they remember to take out the trash without being asked? Boom, celebration time. Did they try a new hairstyle? Time for some positive reinforcement.

Now, I'm not saying you need to throw a parade every time they breathe. But a simple "I noticed you..." can go a long way. "I noticed you helped your sister with her homework. That was really kind of you." Or "I saw how hard you worked on that project, even though it was challenging. I'm proud of you for not giving up."

It can be really fun to surprise your teen with random acts of acknowledgment. Send an unexpected text during the day: "Just thinking about how awesome you are. Have a great day!" Or pop into their room (knock first, unless you want to risk seeing something that'll scar you both for life) just to say, "Hey, I was just thinking about how much I enjoy our talks about [insert their current obsession]. You always have such interesting perspectives."

These random positive reinforcements are like surprise attacks of love. They catch your teen off guard in the best way possible. And even if they roll their eyes or grunt in response, trust me, they're taking it in. It's like emotional nutrition—it's feeding their self-esteem, even if they don't realize it.

Encourage Independence

This one's tricky because it involves us parents doing the hardest thing ever—letting go a little. But remember, the goal is to raise an adult, not a perpetual child.

You can start by giving them age-appropriate responsibilities that help them feel capable and trusted. For younger teens, this might be managing their own morning routine or being in charge of a specific household chore. For older teens, it could be more complex tasks like managing their own schedule or budget.

As an idea, you could let them take charge of a home project. Maybe they want to redecorate their room or build a new piece of furniture. Give them a budget and some basic guidelines, then step back and let them take the lead. Sure, they might end up with a neon green wall or a slightly wobbly bookshelf, but they'll have gained valuable experience in planning, decision-making, and execution.

Or you could set them a challenge, like teaching the family dog a new trick. It gives them a chance to be the authority figure for once, and it's a great lesson in patience and perseverance (for both your teen and the dog).

The key here is to resist the urge to step in and take over when things get tough. Offer guidance if they ask for it, but let them figure things out on their own as much as possible. It's in the struggle that they'll build real confidence.

Modeling Positive Self-Talk

Last but not least, let's talk about the power of positive self-talk. And parents, this one starts with us. Our teens are watching us all the time (even when we think they're not), and they're picking up on how we talk to and about ourselves.

It really helps to share your own experiences of overcoming self-doubt. Next time you're facing a challenge, voice your thought process out loud. "I'm nervous about this presentation at work, but I'm going to prepare thoroughly and do my best. Even if it's not perfect, I'll learn from the experience."

When you make a mistake, model how to handle it with grace and self-compassion. "Oops, I really messed up that recipe. Oh well, everyone makes mistakes sometimes. Let's see what we can learn from this for next time."

Help your teen identify and challenge their negative self-talk. If you hear them say something like "I'm so stupid," gently challenge that thought. "Is that really true? Or is it that this particular task is challenging? Remember when you struggled with [insert past challenge] and then mastered it? This is just another opportunity to grow."

Teach them to reframe negative thoughts into more positive, realistic ones. Instead of "I'm going to fail this test," encourage them to think, "This test is challenging, but I'm going to do my best and learn from the experience."

Managing Emotions

One minute they're on top of the world, the next they're in the depths of despair because their favorite shirt is in the wash. It's enough to give anyone whiplash! Let's see if we can come up with some quick wins for you to help you work through this, shall we?

Teaching Emotional Labeling

This is all about teaching your teen to identify and name what they're feeling. Why? Because putting a name to a feeling can make it less overwhelming and more manageable.

Here's something to try: When your teen is visibly emotional, instead of asking "What's wrong?" (which often leads to the dreaded "Nothing"), try saying something like, "It seems like you're feeling frustrated. Is that right?" This does two things: It shows you're paying attention, and it gives them a starting point to express themselves.

You should also model emotional awareness yourself. Share your own feelings out loud. "I'm feeling a bit anxious about this work deadline, but I know I can handle it." This shows your teen that it's normal and okay to have and express emotions.

Introducing Relaxation Techniques

Next, let's talk about chilling out—literally. Teaching your teen some simple relaxation techniques can be a game-changer when emotions are running high.

Start with some easy breathing exercises. The "4-7-8" technique is a good one: breathe in for 4 counts, hold for 7, exhale for 8. It's like a mini vacation for the brain.

For the more active teens, try some physical stress-busters. A quick workout, a walk around the block, or even an impromptu dance party in the living room can work wonders. The key is to find what works for your teen—one size really doesn't fit all when it comes to stress relief.

Creating an "Emotion Toolkit"

Think of this as your teen's emotional first-aid kit. It's a personalized set of strategies they can use when feelings get overwhelming.

Sit down with your teen and brainstorm what helps them feel better when they're stressed or upset. Maybe it's listening to a specific playlist, drawing, writing in a journal, or playing with a pet. Whatever it is, make sure these tools are easily accessible.

You can even create a physical "calm down box" with items that engage the senses. Include things like stress balls, scented candles, or photos of happy memories. It's like a hug in a box for those tough emotional moments.

Improving Communication

If you get this right, everything else in parenting becomes a whole lot easier. That's not to say you should be aiming for perfection here; simply making progress is great! Here are my top tips for communication:

Active Listening

Become a world-class listener. This means more than just hearing the words coming out of your teen's mouth. It's about showing genuine interest in what they're saying. We've mentioned this one throughout the book because it's just so important. Put your phone down, make eye contact, and really focus on what they're saying. Nod, make encouraging sounds, and watch your body language.

Asking Open-Ended Questions

If you want to get more than one-word answers, then ask better questions. Instead of "How was school?" (cue the "Fine"), try something like "What was the most interesting thing that happened today?" or "Tell me about a moment that made you laugh."

Here are some great conversation starters:

- "If you could change one thing about your day, what would it be?"

- "What's something you're looking forward to this week?"

- "If you could have dinner with any person, living or dead, who would it be and why?"

The key is to avoid questions that can be answered with a simple "yes" or "no." You're aiming for questions that invite stories, opinions, and feelings.

Creating Opportunities for Casual Conversations

Sometimes, the best conversations happen when you're not trying to have a conversation. You really can use everyday moments for meaningful interactions.

Car rides are great for this. There's something about being side-by-side instead of face-to-face that can make teens more comfortable opening up. Plus, they can't really get away unless they want to tuck and roll on to the sidewalk.

Mealtimes are another great chance for connection. Try to have at least a few family dinners each week sans phones and other distractions. You might be surprised at what comes up when you're passing the potatoes.

Good communication isn't about having deep, meaningful conversations every single day. It's about creating an atmosphere where your teen feels comfortable sharing when they need to. You're basically leaving the door open, letting them know you're there whenever they're ready to walk through it.

Encouraging Positive Behavior

You actually can encourage positive behavior without turning your home into a military boot camp or a hippie commune. Let's learn how:

Use Positive Reinforcement

Yep, it can be as simple as praising them. But not just any praise will do—I'm talking about specific, genuine praise that reinforces the behaviors you want to see more of.

Instead of a generic "Good job," try something like, "I really appreciate how you took the initiative to clean up the kitchen without being asked. It shows responsibility and consideration for others." See the difference? You're not just acknowledging the action but also the positive character traits it demonstrates. The only tricky bit is getting them to listen to a whole sentence without walking away.

Now, let's talk about those classic teen behaviors that drive us up the wall—the eye rolls, the grunts, the door slams. Remember, your teen has a circus going on up there, and the world is a confusing place right now. Try not to take it personally. Instead, look for the feelings behind the behavior. That eye roll might actually mean, "I'm feeling overwhelmed and don't know how to express it."

When you spot a positive behavior, even a small one, pounce on it like a cat on a laser pointer. "I noticed you held the door for that elderly neighbor. That was really thoughtful of you."

Set Clear and Consistent Boundaries

Teens might push against boundaries, but deep down, they need and want them. When setting rules, involve your teen in the process. Ask for their input. You might be surprised at how reasonable they can be. Explain the reasoning behind the rules. "We have this curfew because we worry about your safety when you're out late, and you need enough sleep to function well at school."

Be clear about consequences, too, and follow through consistently. If the consequence of missing curfew is not going out the next weekend, stick to it, even if it means missing the social event of the season.

Model Desired Behavior

I've said it many times: Our teens are watching us. All. The. Time. They might act like we're invisible, but trust me, they're taking notes.

Want your teen to be kind? Show kindness. Want them to be responsible? Model responsibility. Want them to manage their emotions well? Let them see you handling stress and frustration in healthy ways.

Share your thought processes out loud. "I'm feeling really frustrated with this work situation, but I'm going to take a deep breath and think about the best way to handle it." You're giving them a play-by-play of emotional regulation in action.

Be willing to admit when you're wrong and apologize. It shows that it's okay to make mistakes and that taking responsibility for them is important. Plus, it makes it easier for them to do the same.

I hope you enjoyed my quick-win bonus chapter. The most important part of all of this is that you start implementing these simple strategies today. Not next week and not when things calm down (because things rarely calm down with teens). Start with one or two of these quick wins and give them a try.

Conclusion

Well, well, well. Look at you. You made it to the end of a parenting book without throwing it across the room in exasperation. There may have been many cups of coffee. You might even have used this book as a pillow on one late-night "Where is my teen?" worry session. But you are still here, standing strong and still striving to be the best parent you can be.

We've been through a lot together here. We looked at the complexities of the teenage boys' mind, explored strategies for resilience and self-esteem, tackled tough topics like addiction and mental health, and even picked up some quick wins for strengthening your relationship.

But if there's one thing I want you to take away from this book, it's this:

You are exactly the parent your son needs.

Yes, you. With all your imperfections, doubts, and moments of frustration. Your willingness to learn and try new approaches are the reasons you are doing such a great job already, despite how you may have felt when you first picked up this book.

The perfect parent doesn't exist (thank *God*, because that person would be insufferable, right?). The goal is to be a present parent, an evolving parent, and a parent who's willing to adapt and learn alongside their child. All the small efforts that you make and the conversations you initiate all add up, along with every moment of empathy you show. With your help, your son is going to grow into an adult with the confidence and skills to do great things in this world.

So, when you close this book and step back into the chaos of parenting, I want you to hold your head high and trust your instincts. Most of all, be patient with yourself and your son. Don't underestimate the power of your love and presence in your son's life.

Now, take a deep breath... smell that? Yeah, we never did get to the bottom of why his room smells like that...

Glossary

Active Listening: A communication technique that involves fully concentrating on, understanding, and responding to the speaker.

Adolescence: The period of physical and psychological development between childhood and adulthood.

Attention Deficit Hyperactivity Disorder (ADHD): A neurodevelopmental disorder characterized by inattention, hyperactivity, and impulsivity.

Amygdala: A part of the brain responsible for processing emotions, particularly fear and aggression.

Autonomy: The state of being self-governing or independent.

Circadian Rhythm: The natural, internal process that regulates the sleep-wake cycle and repeats roughly every 24 hours.

Dopamine: A neurotransmitter associated with pleasure, motivation, and reward.

Emotional Intelligence: The ability to recognize, understand, and manage one's own emotions and the emotions of others.

Empathy: The ability to understand and share the feelings of another.

Growth Mindset: The belief that abilities and intelligence can be developed through effort, learning, and persistence.

Helicopter Parenting: A style of child-rearing in which parents are overly focused on their children's experiences and problems.

Identity Formation: The process of developing a sense of self during adolescence.

Imposter Syndrome: A psychological pattern in which an individual doubts their skills, talents, or accomplishments.

Limbic System: A set of brain structures involved in behavioral and emotional responses, particularly related to survival.

Melatonin: A hormone that regulates the sleep-wake cycle.

Mindfulness: A mental state achieved by focusing one's awareness on the present moment.

Peer Pressure: The influence exerted by a peer group in encouraging a person to change their attitudes, values, or behaviors.

Prefrontal Cortex: The part of the brain responsible for complex cognitive behavior, decision-making, and moderating social behavior.

Resilience: The ability to recover quickly from difficulties; toughness.

Self-Esteem: Confidence in one's own worth or abilities; self-respect.

Self-Harm: Deliberate injury to oneself, typically as a manifestation of a psychological or psychiatric disorder.

Toxic Masculinity: A set of attitudes and ways of behaving, stereotypically associated with men, that are seen as having a negative impact on men and society as a whole.

Validation: The recognition or affirmation that a person or their feelings or opinions are valid or worthwhile.

About the Author

I'm Laura Thomas, and I've been on a wild ride with teenagers for over two decades now. As a psychotherapist with an M.E.d. in Social, Emotional, and Mental Health and a BSc (Hons) in Psychology, I've dedicated my career to understanding and supporting young people and their families since 2003.

I've worn many hats over the years—working in schools, charities, local authorities, and now in my own private practice. I've supported teens from all walks of life, from those in care and youth offending units to gifted students and kids grappling with severe mental health issues. Each experience has taught me something new about the incredible resilience and potential of our young people.

But my most challenging (and rewarding) role? Being a mom to two teenage daughters. Trust me, nothing puts your professional knowledge to the test quite like parenting your own teens, let me tell you!

I love sharing practical skills and advice to help parents through the teenage years. And let's be honest, sometimes we all need a bit of help staying sane through this journey!

My approach? I believe in combining solid, evidence-based techniques with real-world practicality and a healthy dose of humor. Because if we can't laugh about some of this stuff, then we might just cry!

At the end of the day, my goal is to empower parents like you to build strong, lasting connections with your teens while supporting their journey to independence.

When I'm not working with clients or writing, you can often find me adventuring in the great outdoors. I'm a bit of a nature enthusiast, whether I'm taking long walks through the picturesque Bedfordshire countryside or exploring the stunning south coast of the New Forest (a place my family absolutely adores). My faithful companions on these walks are our two dogs, Bailey and Milo, who—unlike my teenage daughters—are always happy to see me!

Since hitting the big 4-0, I've discovered that I have quite the green thumb. My garden has become my sanctuary, and I've developed a slightly embarrassing obsession with houseplants. I love them so much that I've actually named each one—just don't tell me eldest daughter; she caught me saying goodnight to them once, and I've never lived it down!

So, when I'm not knee-deep in teenage drama (professional or personal), you'll likely find me pruning, pottering, and chatting with my leafy friends. It's my way of finding peace and balance in the wonderful chaos that is life with teenagers.

Want to know more about me and my work? Please do check out my website at **www.parentologyworld.com**

LOVED THE BOOK?
YOUR *REVIEW* MEANS THE WORLD!

If you enjoyed this book and found it helpful, I would be so grateful if you could take a moment to **share your thoughts** in a review.

Reviews are incredibly valuable for authors like me, as they help **more parents** discover the book, gain valuable insights, and build a supportive community here at ***Parentology World.***

Scan this code to leave a review!

Your ***honest feedback*** is incredibly valuable to me, and I truly appreciate your time.

Thank you for your support!

Laura

www.parentologyworld.com

PRINTABLE

Don't Forget to Grab Your Teen Their TWO FREE Journals!

These journals are crafted to support your teen's journey in building self-esteem, emotional resilience, and goal-setting skills.

They'll discover tools to manage emotions, set intentions, and grow in confidence.

Let these journals be a gift for them, helping them feel supported every step of the way.

References

Axelrod, A. (2016). *Attention Deficit Hyperactivity Disorder (ADHD)*. Transcendental Meditation. https://uk.tm.org/tm-adhd

Bergland, C. (2017, July 28). *Silent third person self-talk facilitates emotion regulation*. Psychology Today. https://www.psychologytoday.com/gb/blog/the-athletes-way/201707/silent-third-person-self-talk-facilitates-emotion-regulation

Better Help Editorial Team. (2024, June 2). *Exploring the impact of masking emotions on men's mental health*. Better Help. https://www.betterhelp.com/advice/mental-health-of-men-and-boys/exploring-the-impact-of-masking-emotions-on-mens-mental-health/

Brain development in pre-teens and teenagers. (2021). Raising Children Network. https://raisingchildren.net.au/pre-teens/development/understanding-your-pre-teen/brain-development-teens

Cherry, K. (2023, December 31). *5 key components of emotional intelligence*. Verywell Mind. https://www.verywellmind.com/components-of-emotional-intelligence-2795438

Ciccia, A. H., Meulenbroek, P., & Turkstra, L. S. (2009). Adolescent brain and cognitive developments. *Topics in Language Disorders, 29*(3), 249–265. https://doi.org/10.1097/tld.0b013e3181b53211

Cleveland Clinic. (2022, May 27). *Video game addiction: What it is, symptoms & treatment*. https://my.clevelandclinic.org/health/diseases/23124-video-game-addiction

Cleveland Clinic. (2023). *Adolescent development*. https://my.clevelandclinic.org/health/articles/7060-adolescent-development

Coca, G., & Wikle, J. (2024). *What happens when children are exposed to pornography?* Institute for Family Studies. https://ifstudies.org/blog/what-happens-when-children-are-exposed-to-pornography

Common signs & symptoms of addiction. (2019). Prioryg Goup. https://www.priorygroup.com/addiction-treatment/signs-and-symptoms-of-addiction

Conflict management with pre-teens and teenagers. (n.d.). Raising Children Network. https://raisingchildren.net.au/teens/communicating-relationships/communicating/conflict-management-with-teens

Cuncic, A. (2024, February 12). *7 active listening techniques for better communication.* Verywell Mind. https://www.verywellmind.com/what-is-active-listening-3024343

Danial, J. (2020, November 16). *Teenage friendships: Why are they so important?* Simi Psychological Group. https://simipsychologicalgroup.com/teenage-friendships-why-are-they-so-important/

Davis, A. (2022, December 6). *Sexual addiction in teenagers: Understanding the chemistry behind it.* Clearfork Academy. https://clearforkacademy.com/blog/sexual-addiction-in-teenagers

Dealing with anger – for 11-18 year olds. (2021, March). Mind. https://www.mind.org.uk/for-young-people/feelings-and-experiences/dealing-with-anger/#WhyDoIGetAngry

Dent, M. (2020, October 9). Seven tips for parenting teen boys: "Nagging them is like shouting into a void." *The Guardian.* https://www.theguardian.com/lifeandstyle/2020/oct/10/seven-tips-for-parenting-teen-boys-nagging-them-is-like-shouting-into-a-void

Development of self. (n.d.). Lumen. https://courses.lumenlearning.com/child/chapter/development-of-self-2/

Domestic abuse. (2024). Victim Support. https://www.victimsupport.org.uk/crime-info/types-crime/domestic-abuse/

Environmental factors impacting teen mental health. (2024, March 11). Adolescent Wellness Academy. https://adolescentwellnessacademy.com/teen-mental-health/main-causes/environmental-factors/

França, T. F. A., & Pompeia, S. (2023). Reappraising the role of dopamine in adolescent risk-taking behavior. *Neuroscience & Biobehavioral Reviews, 147*, 105085. https://doi.org/10.1016/j.neubiorev.2023.105085

Galvan, A. (2010). Adolescent development of the reward system. *Frontiers in Human Neuroscience, 4*(6). https://doi.org/10.3389/neuro.09.006.2010

Griffith University. (2014). *Physical, social, emotional and cognitive development.* FutureLearn. https://www.futurelearn.com/info/courses/supporting-adolescent-learners/0/steps/46451

Hagenauer, M. H., Perryman, J. I., Lee, T. M., & Carskadon, M. A. (2009). Adolescent changes in the homeostatic and circadian regulation of sleep. *Developmental Neuroscience, 31*(4), 276–284. https://doi.org/10.1159/000216538

How social media shapes unrealistic expectations in children. (2023, August 29). Safes. https://www.safes.so/blogs/unrealistic-expectations-in-children/

The importance of emotional literacy and how to improve yours. (2021). Clare & Me. https://www.clareandme.com/post/the-importance-of-emotional-literacy-and-how-to-improve-yours

It's good for everyone when boys can be vulnerable. (2022, September 8). CBE International. https://www.cbeinternational.org/resource/its-good-everyone-when-boys-can-be-vulnerable/

kirriliesmout. (2015, March 31). *The teen grunt: Getting teens and preteens to speak politely.* Developing Minds. https://developingminds.net.au/blog/2015/4/29/the-teen-grunt-getting-teens-and-preteens-to-speak-politely.html

Lehman, J. (2024, April 18). *Does your child have toxic friends? How to deal with the wrong crowd.* Empowering Parents.com. https://www.empoweringparents.com/article/does-your-child-have-toxic-friends-6-ways-to-deal-with-the-wrong-crowd

Lonczak, H. (2020, December 24). *How to express your emotions in A healthy way: 30 practical tips.* PositivePsychology.com. https://positivepsychology.com/express-emotions/

Martelo, C. (2023, October 18). *What is positive parenting self-reflection?* Huckleberry. https://huckleberrycare.com/blog/what-is-positive-parenting-self-reflection

Mastroianni, B. (2022, November 30). *Addressing boys' mental health.* Charlie Health. https://www.charliehealth.com/post/addressing-boys-mental-health

McKean, A. (2023, March 1). *When children and teens self-harm.* HealthyChildren.org. https://www.healthychildren.org/English/health-issues/conditions/emotional-problems/Pages/when-children-and-teens-self-harm.aspx

Monroe, J. (2012, December 15). *The effects of teenage hormones on adolescent emotions.* Newport Academy. https://www.newportacademy.com/resources/empowering-teens/teenage-hormones-and-sexuality/

Murdock, A. (2020, March 25). *The evolutionary advantage of the teenage brain.* University of California. https://www.universityofcalifornia.edu/news/evolutionary-advantage-teenage-brain

Myler, C. (2020, July 27). *Understanding teen boys' anger.* Maggie Dent. https://www.maggiedent.com/blog/understanding-teen-boys-anger/

National Institute on Alcohol Abuse and Alcoholism. (2022). *Alcohol's effects on health.* https://www.niaaa.nih.gov/publications/alcohol-and-brain-overview

National Institute on Drug Abuse. (2011, July). *Drugs and the brain.* https://nida.nih.gov/publications/drugs-brains-behavior-science-addiction/drugs-brain

National Institute on Drug Abuse. (2020, July). *Drug misuse and addiction.* https://nida.nih.gov/publications/drugs-brains-behavior-science-addiction/drug-misuse-addiction

National Institute of Mental Health. (2024, February). *Caring for your mental health.* https://www.nimh.nih.gov/health/topics/caring-for-your-mental-health

9 ways to boost your child's self-esteem (for parents). (2023, September). Nemours KidsHealth. https://kidshealth.org/en/parents/boost-self-esteem.html

The Partnership. (2017, February). *Why teens drink and experiment with drugs: Top 8 reasons.* Partnership to End Addiction. https://drugfree.org/article/why-teens-drink-and-experiment-with-drugs/

Pizzini, N. (2015, September 15). *Grunts and eye rolls, finding a better way to communicate.* Narrative Pathways. https://narrativepathways.com/grunts-and-eye-rolls-finding-a-better-way-to-communicate/

Promises Behavioral Health. (2022, November 21). *6 reasons men keep their depression a secret.* https://www.promises.com/addiction-blog/6-reasons-men-keep-depression-secret/

Ragelienė, T. (2016). Links of adolescents identity development and relationship with peers: A systematic literature review. *Journal of the Canadian Academy of Child and Adolescent Psychiatry, 25*(2), 97–105. https://www.ncbi.nlm.nih.gov/pmc/articles/PMC4879949/

Recognizing the subtle signs of mental health challenges. (2024). Psych Company. https://www.psychcompany.com/2024/recognizing-the-subtle-signs-of-mental-health-challenges/

Romer, D. (2010). Adolescent risk taking, impulsivity, and brain development: Implications for prevention. *Developmental Psychobiology, 52*(3). https://doi.org/10.1002/dev.20442

Setting expectations for teen. (2024). Children's Healthcare Associates. https://www.chapeds.com/blog/1134889-setting-realistic-expectations-for-teens/

Stanborough, R., J. (2021, March 30). *ADHD and anger: How they are connected.* Healthline. https://www.healthline.com/health/adhd/adhd-and-anger#in-daily-life

The teen brain: 7 things to know. (2020). National Institute of Mental Health. https://www.nimh.nih.gov/health/publications/the-teen-brain-7-things-to-know

Toussaint, K. (2014, November 1). *When your good kid has bad friends.* Teen Therapy Center. https://teentherapycenter.com/when-your-good-kid-has-bad-friends/

Tran, R. (2021, February 14). *Media romances skew real-world relationship standards.* UCSD Guardian. https://ucsdguardian.org/2021/02/14/media-romances-skew-real-world-relationship-standards/

van Schoor, J. (2023, June 28). *Understanding the key stages of childhood development.* SACAP Global. https://global.sacap.edu.za/blog/applied-psychology/understanding-key-stages-in-childhood-development/

von der Heiden, J. M., Braun, B., Müller, K. W., & Egloff, B. (2019). The association between video gaming and psychological functioning. *Frontiers in Psychology, 10*(1731). https://www.frontiersin.org/articles/10.3389/fpsyg.2019.01731/full

What the science tells us about adolescent sleep. (n.d.). UCLA Center for the Developing Adolescent. https://developingadolescent.semel.ucla.edu/topics/item/science-of-adolescent-sleep

Why your children really should play videogames. (2023). Iberdrola. https://www.iberdrola.com/talent/benefits-video-games-learning

Yeager, D. S., & Dweck, C. S. (2020). What can be learned from growth mindset controversies? *American Psychologist, 75*(9), 1269–1284. https://doi.org/10.1037/amp0000794

Printed in Dunstable, United Kingdom